WESTCHESTER PUBLIC LIB.

W9-CKH-877

3 1310 00228 4194

DISCARD

PROTECTING YOUR BUSINESS: DISASTER PREPARATION AND THE LAW

by

Margaret C. Jasper

Oceana's Legal Almanac Series:
Law for the Layperson

Oceana®
NEW YORK

658.477
Jas

OXFORD
UNIVERSITY PRESS

*Oxford University Press, Inc., publishes works that further Oxford University's
objective of excellence in research, scholarship, and education.*

Copyright © 2008 by Oxford University Press, Inc.
Published by Oxford University Press, Inc.
198 Madison Avenue, New York, New York 10016

Oxford is a registered trademark of Oxford University Press
Oceana is a registered trademark of Oxford University Press, Inc.

All rights reserved. No part of this publication may be reproduced, stored in a
retrieval system, or transmitted, in any form or by any means, electronic,
mechanical, photocopying, recording, or otherwise, without the prior
permission of Oxford University Press, Inc.

Library of Congress Cataloging-in-Publication Data

Jasper, Margaret C.
  Protecting your business : disaster preparation and the law / by
Margaret C. Jasper.
    p. cm. — (Oceana's legal almanac series: law for the layperson) Includes
bibliographic references.
  ISBN: 978-0-19-533903-1 ((clothbound) : alk. paper)   1. Emergency
management — United States. 2. Small business — Security measures —
United States.   3. Insurance, Business—United States.   4. Disaster relief—
United States.   I. Title
  HV551.3.J37 2007
  658.4'77—dc22   2007030689

Note to Readers:
This publication is designed to provide accurate and authoritative information in
regard to the subject matter covered. It is based upon sources believed to be accurate and reliable and is intended to be current as of the time it was written. It is sold
with the understanding that the publisher is not engaged in rendering legal,
accounting, or other professional services. If legal advice or other expert assistance
is required, the services of a competent professional person should be sought. Also,
to confirm that the information has not been affected or changed by recent develop-
ments, traditional legal research techniques should be used, including checking
primary sources where appropriate.

*(Based on the Declaration of Principles jointly adopted by a Committee of the
American Bar Association and a Committee of Publishers and Associations.)*

You may order this or any other Oxford University Press publication
by visiting the Oxford University Press web site at www.oup.com

To My Husband Chris

Your love and support

are my motivation and inspiration

To my sons, Michael, Nick and Chris

-and-

In memory of my son, Jimmy

Table of Contents

ABOUT THE AUTHOR vii

INTRODUCTION x

CHAPTER 1:
EMERGENCY MANAGEMENT PLANNING

IN GENERAL 1
FORM AN EMERGENCY MANAGEMENT TEAM 2
ASSESS YOUR CURRENT RISKS 2
   Previous Incidents 3
   Geographic Risks 3
   Technological Risks 3
   Human Error 4
   Design and Construction Emergencies 4
   Plan for Specific Types of Emergency Situations 4
DETERMINE POTENTIAL IMPACT 5
   Human Impact 5
   Impact on Business Operations 5
   Impact on Facility and Property 5
ESTABLISH TIMELINES AND BUDGETS 5
REVIEW EXISTING PLANS 6
ESTABLISH A BACKUP PLAN 6
DESIGNATE STAGING AREAS 7
DETERMINE COMMUNITY RESOURCES 7
DETERMINE CODES AND REGULATIONS 8
THE FEDERAL EMERGENCY MANAGEMENT AGENCY 8

CHAPTER 2:
DEVELOPING AND IMPLEMENTING THE
EMERGENCY PLAN

PLAN COMPONENTS 9
Executive Summary 9
Emergency Response Procedures. 9
Emergency Contact Information. 10
Building Plans and Maps 10
WRITING THE PLAN 10
IMPLEMENTING YOUR EMERGENCY
MANAGEMENT PLAN. 11
NOTIFICATION AND WARNING SYSTEM 11
EVACUATION PLANNING 12
High Rise Buildings 13
SHELTER 13
EQUIPMENT AND DATA PROTECTION. 13
Equipment Protection 14
Maintain an Inventory 14
Data Protection and Storage 15
PUBLIC INFORMATION AND MEDIA RELATIONS 15
MEDICAL EMERGENCIES 16
First Aid Supplies. 16
Food 17
Water. 17
Medications. 17
Miscellaneous Items 17
EMERGENCY MANAGEMENT COSTS. 18
EMPLOYEES AND THEIR FAMILIES 18

CHAPTER 3:
PLANNING FOR SPECIFIC DISASTERS

IN GENERAL 19
FIRES 19
Planning Considerations – Fires 19
HAZARDOUS MATERIALS 21
Hazardous Materials Regulation 21
Planning Considerations – Hazardous Materials 22
Off-Site Incidents. 22
FLOODS 24
Planning Considerations – Floods 24
HURRICANES 25
Planning Considerations – Hurricanes 25

TORNADOES 26
  Planning Considerations – Tornadoes 26
SEVERE WINTER STORMS 27
  Planning Considerations – Severe Winter Storms 27
EARTHQUAKES 28
  Planning Considerations – Earthquakes 28
TECHNOLOGICAL EMERGENCIES 29
  Planning Considerations – Technological Emergencies 30

CHAPTER 4:
PREPARING YOUR WORKPLACE FOR A PANDEMIC
WHAT IS A PANDEMIC? 31
EFFECT OF A PANDEMIC ON BUSINESS OPERATIONS 32
ROLE OF THE EMPLOYER 32
LEVEL OF RISK 32
PLANNING CONSIDERATIONS 33
  Community Planning 33
  Review Your Emergency Plan Regularly 33
  Contingency Planning 33
  Identify and Minimize Risks 34
  Assist Employees in Crisis 34
EMPLOYEES WHO TRAVEL OUTSIDE THE UNITED STATES 34

CHAPTER 5:
BUSINESS INSURANCE
IN GENERAL 37
BUSINESS OWNERS POLICY 38
PROPERTY INSURANCE 39
  Exclusions 39
    Flood Coverage 39
    Earthquake Coverage 40
    Acts of Terrorism 40
BUSINESS INTERRUPTION INSURANCE 41
  Named Perils Policy 42
  All-Risk Policy 42
  Extra Expense Insurance 43
FILING YOUR INSURANCE CLAIM 43
POLICY CANCELLATION 43
POLICY NONRENEWAL 43
FILING A COMPLAINT AGAINST YOUR INSURANCE CARRIER 44

CHAPTER 6:
DAMAGE ASSESSMENT AND RECOVERY

IN GENERAL 45
DAMAGE ASSESSMENT 45
FINANCING YOUR RECOVERY 46
GETTING BACK TO BUSINESS 47
ASSISTING YOUR EMPLOYEES 48

CHAPTER 7:
THE SMALL BUSINESS ADMINISTRATION
DISASTER RELIEF LOAN PROGRAM

IN GENERAL 49
APPLYING FOR FINANCIAL ASSISTANCE 49
USE OF FUNDS 50
  Physical Damage 50
  Economic Injury. 51
LOAN TERMS 52
THE MILITARY RESERVIST ECONOMIC
INJURY DISASTER LOAN PROGRAM 52
  Use of Funds 53
  Loan Terms 53
  Documentation 54
THE SBA DISASTER OFFICE 54
  The SBA Disaster Assistance
  Customer Service Center 54
  The SBA Field Operations Center – East (FOC-E) 55
  The SBA Field Operations Center – West (FOC-W) 55
  The SBA Disaster Assistance Processing
  and Disbursement Center 56

APPENDICES

1: DIRECTORY OF FEDERAL EMERGENCY
   MANAGEMENT AGENCY – REGIONAL OFFICES 57
2: DIRECTORY OF STATE OFFICES
   OF EMERGENCY MANAGEMENT 59
3: BUSINESS CONTINUITY ACRONYMS 67
4: SAMPLE EMERGENCY PLAN. 73
5: EMERGENCY SUPPLIES CHECKLIST 81
6: COMPUTER INVENTORY FORM. 83
7: LIST OF HAZARDOUS CHEMICALS. 85
8: CHECKLIST FOR PANDEMIC PLANNING 91
9: INSURANCE COVERAGE DISCUSSION FORM 95

10: SELECTED PROVISIONS OF THE TERRORISM RISK
   INSURANCE ACT OF 2002 AND THE TERRORISM RISK
   INSURANCE EXTENSION ACT OF 2005 97
11: DIRECTORY OF STATE INSURANCE DEPARTMENTS 109
12: U.S. SBA DISASTER BUSINESS LOAN APPLICATION 115

GLOSSARY 117

BIBLIOGRAPHY AND ADDITIONAL RESOURCES 135

ABOUT THE AUTHOR

MARGARET C. JASPER is an attorney engaged in the general practice of law in South Salem, New York, concentrating in the areas of personal injury and entertainment law. Ms. Jasper holds a Juris Doctor degree from Pace University School of Law, White Plains, New York, is a member of the New York and Connecticut bars, and is certified to practice before the United States District Courts for the Southern and Eastern Districts of New York, the United States Court of Appeals for the Second Circuit, and the United States Supreme Court.

Ms. Jasper has been appointed to the law guardian panel for the Family Court of the State of New York, is a member of a number of professional organizations and associations, and is a New York State licensed real estate broker operating as Jasper Real Estate, in South Salem, New York.

Margaret Jasper maintains a website at http://www.JasperLawOffice.com.

In 2004, Ms. Jasper successfully argued a case before the New York Court of Appeals, which gives mothers of babies who are stillborn due to medical negligence the right to bring a legal action and recover emotional distress damages. This successful appeal overturned a 26-year old New York case precedent, which previously prevented mothers of stillborn babies from suing their negligent medical providers.

Ms. Jasper is the author and general editor of the following legal almanacs:

AIDS Law
The Americans with Disabilities Act
Animal Rights Law
Auto Leasing
Bankruptcy Law for the Individual Debtor
Banks and their Customers
Becoming a Citizen
Buying and Selling Your Home

Commercial Law
Consumer Rights and the Law
Co-ops and Condominiums: Your Rights and Obligations As Owner
Copyright Law
Credit Cards and the Law
Custodial Rights
Dealing with Debt
Dictionary of Selected Legal Terms
Drunk Driving Law
DWI, DUI and the Law
Education Law
Elder Law
Employee Rights in the Workplace
Employment Discrimination Under Title VII
Environmental Law
Estate Planning
Everyday Legal Forms
Executors and Personal Representatives: Rights and Responsibilities
Harassment in the Workplace
Health Care and Your Rights
Health Care Directives
Hiring Household Help and Contractors: Your Rights and Obligations
Under the Law
Home Mortgage Law Primer
Hospital Liability Law
How To Change Your Name
How To Form an LLC
How To Protect Your Challenged Child
How To Start Your Own Business
Identity Theft and How To Protect Yourself
Individual Bankruptcy and Restructuring
Injured on the Job: Employee Rights, Worker's Compensation and
Disability Insurance Law
International Adoption
Juvenile Justice and Children's Law
Labor Law
Landlord-Tenant Law
Law for the Small Business Owner
The Law of Attachment and Garnishment
The Law of Buying and Selling
The Law of Capital Punishment
The Law of Child Custody
The Law of Contracts
The Law of Debt Collection

The Law of Dispute Resolution
The Law of Immigration
The Law of Libel and Slander
The Law of Medical Malpractice
The Law of No-Fault Insurance
The Law of Obscenity and Pornography
The Law of Personal Injury
The Law of Premises Liability
The Law of Product Liability
The Law of Speech and the First Amendment
Lemon Laws
Living Together: Practical Legal Issues
Marriage and Divorce
Missing and Exploited Children: How to Protect Your Child
Motor Vehicle Law
Nursing Home Negligence
Patent Law
Pet Law
Prescription Drugs
Privacy and the Internet: Your Rights and Expectations Under the Law
Probate Law
Protecting Your Business: Disaster Preparation and the Law
Real Estate Law for the Homeowner and Broker
Religion and the Law
Retirement Planning
The Right to Die
Rights of Single Parents
Small Claims Court
Social Security Law
Special Education Law
Teenagers and Substance Abuse
Trademark Law
Trouble Next Door: What to do With Your Neighbor
Victim's Rights Law
Violence Against Women
Welfare: Your Rights and the Law
What if It Happened to You: Violent Crimes and Victims' Rights
What if the Product Doesn't Work: Warranties & Guarantees
Workers' Compensation Law
Your Child's Legal Rights: An Overview
Your Rights in a Class Action Suit
Your Rights as a Tenant
Your Rights Under the Family and Medical Leave Act
You've Been Fired: Your Rights and Remedies

INTRODUCTION

Be Prepared! How quickly can your company recover following a fire, flood, terrorist attack or other unexpected emergency? The key to recovery is preparedness. If you are committed to emergency planning, your company will be more likely to survive, and your business will have a better chance of recovery.

The resilience of America's businesses is critical to this nation's economy. Small business accounts for more than 99% of all companies with employees. Therefore, it is vital to the security of this country that businesses are able to withstand and rebound from any type of disaster or emergency.

This Almanac provides the business owner with the information necessary to put together a plan that will improve the chances that their company will stay in business in the face of a major disaster. This Almanac also discusses business continuity planning, crisis assessment and management, insurance issues, equipment and data protection, employee preparedness, and sets forth practical measures that will help the business owner prepare for and survive a disaster, and recover as quickly as possible.

The Appendix provides applicable statutes, resource directories, and other pertinent information and data. The Glossary contains definitions of many of the terms used throughout the Almanac.

CHAPTER 1:
EMERGENCY MANAGEMENT PLANNING

IN GENERAL

According to the Federal Emergency Management Agency (FEMA), the number of declared major disasters in the United States has more than doubled, with 529 major disasters occurring from 1995-2004, a 68 percent increase over the number declared in the previous decade.

Whether natural or man-made, disasters take an enormous toll on businesses each year. Although it may be impossible to avoid these events, you can try to minimize the damages by planning ahead. Businesses must create and maintain a comprehensive emergency management program in order to deal with emergency situations.

A workplace emergency is basically defined as any unplanned event that can cause death or significant injury to employees, customers or the public; or that can shut down your business, disrupt operations, cause physical or environmental damage, or threaten the business's financial standing or public image. A disaster can strike at anytime, anywhere, and may include a fire, flood, hurricane, tornado, blizzard, earthquake, pandemic, an act of nature or an act of terrorism, etc., any one of which can be disastrous to a business, particularly a small business.

A responsible company will prepare for a disaster through careful planning. If you are a small business owner, being prepared can mean staying in business following a disaster. According to the Small Business Administration, an estimated 25 percent of businesses do not reopen following a major disaster.

Though every situation is unique, any business can be better prepared if it puts emergency procedures in place, and practices for all kinds of disasters. By careful planning, you will be protecting your business investment and giving your company a better chance for survival.

FORM AN EMERGENCY MANAGEMENT TEAM

In order to develop an adequate emergency plan, you should solicit input from your staff to make sure you cover all of the important issues. Involving your staff is helpful because it encourages participation and lets you know whether any staff members have expertise in various critical areas.

For example, you may discover you have an employee who is a volunteer firefighter in their free time, or one who has some degree of medical expertise that would be helpful in the event of an emergency. In addition, you will be able to determine which staff members are most willing to take an active part in the emergency planning process.

Once you have put together an emergency planning team, each member should be given a particular planning task, e.g., evacuation routes, fire safety, medical supplies, etc. One person should be given overall authority over the group. This can be the business owner, or the person who has the most expertise in emergency planning.

Once the emergency planning team is formed, the purpose of the plan and the authority and structure of the planning team should be put in writing and distributed to all employees to demonstrate the company's commitment to providing a safe and healthy workplace environment. In addition, employees will know who to go to if they have a specific safety concern.

ASSESS YOUR CURRENT RISKS

One of the first things the team should address is the company's vulnerability to particular types of disasters, e.g., natural, man-made, etc. For example, if your business is located in a flood zone, the team should concentrate on planning for flood damage prevention and control as the first priority, and address other issues according to the degree of risk, eventually covering all possibilities.

If you aren't sure whether your business is at risk of a disaster caused by a natural hazard, you can check with your local building official, city engineer, or planning and zoning administrator. They can tell you whether you are in an area where hurricanes, floods, earthquakes, wildfires, or tornadoes are likely to occur. Once you have identified possible hazards and emergencies, you will be better able to prepare for the particular type of risk involved.

Even if you think you are not at risk for a natural disaster in your area, a man-made disaster, such as a hazardous materials spill or a massive power outage, can occur and seriously interrupt your business activities. And, of course, the events of September 11, 2001 demonstrate how quickly things can change at a time and in a place when there was no perceived risk.

The following checklist will assist you in determining your vulnerability for specific types of emergencies.

Previous Incidents

Determine the types of emergencies that have previously occurred in your community, at your facility, and at other facilities in the area, including:

1. Fires;
2. Severe weather;
3. Hazardous material spills;
4. Transportation accidents;
5. Earthquakes;
6. Hurricanes;
7. Tornadoes;
8. Utility outages; and
9. Acts of terrorism.

Geographic Risks

Determine vulnerability based on the location of your facility, including:

1. Proximity to flood plains, seismic faults and dams;
2. Proximity to companies that produce, store, use or transport hazardous materials;
3. Proximity to major transportation routes and airports; and
4. Proximity to nuclear power plants.

Technological Risks

Determine your company's risk if there are certain system failures, including:

1. Fire, explosion, or hazardous materials incident;
2. Safety system failure;
3. Telecommunications failure;
4. Computer system failure;
5. Power failure;
6. Heating/cooling system failure; and
7. Emergency notification system failure.

Human Error

Determine the types of emergencies that can result from employee error. According to FEMA, human error is the single largest cause of workplace emergencies, and can result from:

1. Poor training;

2. Poor maintenance;

3. Carelessness;

4. Misconduct;

5. Substance abuse; and

6. Fatigue.

Design and Construction Emergencies

Determine the types of emergencies that could result from the design and construction of your facility, including:

1. The physical construction of the facility;

2. Hazardous processes or byproducts;

3. Facilities for storing combustibles;

4. Layout of equipment;

5. Lighting;

6. Evacuation routes and exits; and

7. Proximity of shelter areas.

Plan for Specific Types of Emergency Situations

It is important to analyze each potential emergency from beginning to end under various scenarios, including:

1. Loss of electric power;

2. Downed communication lines;

3. Ruptured gas mains;

4. Water damage;

5. Smoke damage;

6. Structural damage;

7. Air or water contamination;

8. Explosion;

9. Building collapse;

10. Trapped persons; and

11. Chemical release.

DETERMINE POTENTIAL IMPACT

In order to set priorities, you must determine the potential impact of each type of emergency situation on your employees, your business operations, and your facility.

Human Impact

Analyze the potential human impact of each emergency, including the possibility of death or injury.

Impact on Business Operations

Analyze the potential impact of each emergency on your business operations, including:

1. Business interruption;

2. Employees unable to report to work;

3. Customers unable to reach your facility;

4. Company in violation of contractual agreements;

5. Imposition of fines and penalties or legal costs;

6. Interruption of critical supplies;

7. Interruption of product distribution; and

8. Loss of market share.

Impact on Facility and Property

You must consider the potential impact of an emergency on your facility and property, including:

1. Replacement costs;

2. Temporary replacement costs; and

3. Repair and rehabilitation costs.

ESTABLISH TIMELINES AND BUDGETS

The emergency management team should set goals and establish timelines according to the known priorities. For example, if there is no evacuation plan currently in place, this would be a priority task that the team should address early on in the planning phase.

In addition, an initial budget should be established for equipment and supplies, and other necessary expenses. For example, equipment that may be needed in an emergency includes:

1. Fire protection and suppression equipment;

2. Communications equipment;

3. First aid supplies;

4. Emergency supplies;

5. Warning systems;

6. Emergency power equipment; and

7. Decontamination equipment, etc.

REVIEW EXISTING PLANS

The emergency management team should review any existing emergency plans and policies so that they can be updated, as needed. This may include the following documents:

1. Evacuation plan;

2. Fire safety plan;

3. Health and safety plan;

4. Hazardous materials plan;

5. Insurance policies; etc.

You should meet with your insurance carrier to review all of your current policies and determine coverages in case you need to update your policies.

ESTABLISH A BACKUP PLAN

A plan to backup company operations during an emergency should be put in place. For example, arrangements could be made with outside facilities to handle the following internal operations:

1. Payroll;

2. Billing;

3. Communications;

4. Manufacture and production;

5. Customer service;

6. Shipping and receiving; and

7. Information systems and technical support, etc.

DESIGNATE STAGING AREAS

In the event that evacuation of the facility is not advisable, areas of the facility should be designated as staging areas in case of emergency, including:

1. An emergency control and information center;

2. Food and shelter areas;

3. First aid stations; and

4. Sanitation facilities, etc.

The emergency control and information center should be located in an area that is not affected by the incident. The following resources should be located in the center:

1. Communications equipment;

2. A copy of the emergency management plan;

3. The facility map;

4. Contact information for the emergency management team members and a description of their duties;

5. Building security system information;

6. Telephone directories;

7. Backup power; and

8. Emergency supplies.

DETERMINE COMMUNITY RESOURCES

Another important step in emergency planning is to determine which outside resources you can turn to in the event of an emergency. This may include:

1. Local and state police;

2. Fire department;

3. Local hospital and ambulance service;

4. Hazardous materials response team;

5. Local FEMA or state emergency management agency;

6. Local American Red Cross chapter;

7. National weather service;

8. Utility companies, etc.

These agencies often publish important disaster planning material and are a source of valuable information.

A list of all of these resources and contact numbers should be printed and distributed to all members of the emergency planning team and staff members, and a copy kept in the company's emergency management folder. A copy should also be posted on an employee bulletin board or other easily accessible area.

DETERMINE CODES AND REGULATIONS

All applicable federal, state and local codes and regulations should be identified and copies of the laws kept in the company's emergency management folder for review as needed. Such rules and regulations may include:

1. Occupational safety and health regulations;

2. Environmental regulations;

3. Zoning regulations;

4. Transportation regulations;

5. Fire safety codes; and

6. Seismic safety codes.

THE FEDERAL EMERGENCY MANAGEMENT AGENCY

The Federal Emergency Management Agency (FEMA) is a government agency under the jurisdiction of the U.S. Department of Homeland Security (DHS). The primary mission of FEMA is to reduce the loss of life and property, and protect the nation from all hazards, including natural disasters, acts of terrorism, and other man-made disasters, by leading and supporting the nation in a risk-based, comprehensive emergency management system of preparedness, protection, response, recovery, and mitigation.

FEMA has more than 2,600 full time employees that work at FEMA headquarters in Washington D.C., at regional and area offices across the country. FEMA also has approximately 4,000 standby disaster assistance employees who are available for deployment after disasters. FEMA often works in partnership with other organizations that are part of the nation's emergency management system. These partners include state and local emergency management agencies, 27 federal agencies and the American Red Cross.

A directory of FEMA Regional Offices is set forth in Appendix 1, and a directory of State Offices of Emergency Management is set forth in Appendix 2. A list of business continuity acronyms used by emergency management personnel is set forth in Appendix 3.

CHAPTER 2:
DEVELOPING AND IMPLEMENTING THE EMERGENCY PLAN

PLAN COMPONENTS

Once you have your emergency management team in place, and have assessed your company's risks and capabilities, you should develop a written emergency management plan. Your emergency plan should include the following basic components.

Executive Summary

The executive summary sets forth a brief overview of the purpose of the plan; the company's emergency management policy; the responsibilities of key personnel; the types of emergencies that could occur; and where emergency response operations will be managed.

Emergency Response Procedures

This section sets forth the emergency response procedures your company will follow when it responds to an emergency situation, including:

1. Assessing the situation and managing response activities, including activating and operating an emergency operations center.

2. Protecting employees, customers, visitors, equipment, vital records and other assets, including: (i) warning employees and customers, (ii) communicating with personnel and community responders; (iii) evacuating the facility and (iv) accounting for all persons who were in the facility.

3. Restoring business operations, including: (i) repair and rehabilitation; (ii) restoring utilities; (iii) processing insurance claims; and (iv) obtaining necessary disaster financing.

This section should also describe procedures needed to address specific emergency situations, such as an earthquake, fire, or toxic chemical spill, and a list of equipment, supplies and services that may be needed.

Emergency Contact Information

This section should include contact information that may be needed in an emergency, including:

1. Emergency Management Team – The names and contact information for all members of the emergency management team and any other persons who would be involved in responding to an emergency, detailing their roles and responsibilities.

2. Community Resources – Contact information for all community resources available to assist in an emergency, including local and state police; fire department; local hospital and ambulance service; hazardous materials response team; local FEMA or state emergency management agency; local American Red Cross chapter; national weather service; insurance agents; utility companies, etc.

Building Plans and Maps

This section should contain a map that clearly sets forth the location of utility shutoff valves, water hydrants, main water valves, gas main valves, gas lines, electrical substations, storm drains, sewer lines, floor plans, fire alarms, fire extinguishers, fire suppression systems, exits, stairways, elevators shafts, emergency escape routes, restricted areas, hazardous materials, and inventory, etc.

WRITING THE PLAN

Each member of the emergency management team should be responsible for researching and writing a section of the plan, according to a set deadline. Establish a schedule for completion of (1) a first draft; (2) a review and discussion of the first draft; (3) a second draft; (4) a review and discussion of the second draft; (5) the final draft; (6) printing; and (7) distribution.

Consider meeting with representatives of outside agencies, such as your local FEMA or state emergency management agency, local police department, and fire department, to gather their input which may prove useful in developing your plan.

Copies of the final plan should be distributed to key personnel, including management and members of the emergency management team, who should also keep a copy of the plan at home. A copy of the plan should also be kept at company headquarters.

A sample emergency plan is set forth in Appendix 4.

IMPLEMENTING YOUR EMERGENCY MANAGEMENT PLAN

Once the plan has been finalized, you should advise company employees about the plan and establish a training schedule to make sure the plan is workable before it is formally adopted and implemented. You should not wait until an emergency arises to test your plan.

Every individual who works at or regularly visits your company's facility requires some form of training. Assign responsibility for developing a training plan to a member of the emergency management team. Training can be carried out in a number of ways, including:

1. Orientation and Education Sessions - These are regularly scheduled discussion sessions to provide information, answer questions and identify needs and concerns.

2. Discussion - Members of the emergency management team meet to discuss their responsibilities and how they would react to emergency scenarios.

3. Practice Drill - The emergency management team actually performs their emergency response functions.

4. Functional Drills - These drills test specific functions such as medical response, emergency notifications, warning and communications procedures and equipment.

5. Evacuation Drill - Personnel walk the evacuation route to a designated area where procedures for accounting for all personnel are tested.

6. Full-Scale Exercise - A real-life emergency situation is simulated as closely as possible. This exercise involves company emergency response personnel, employees, management and community response organizations.

After the plan has been tested, any problems should be evaluated and, if necessary, the plan should be modified accordingly. Regular review of the emergency plan is advised, particularly if there are any major changes that may impact the effectiveness of the plan, e.g., major changes in personnel, or a change in the design or layout of the company's facility.

NOTIFICATION AND WARNING SYSTEM

Procedures should be established for employees to report an emergency in the facility. Emergency telephone numbers should be posted in prominent locations around the facility, including employee bulletin boards and at telephone stations.

Establish a warning system for employees in case of an emergency, such as a public address system. The warning system should be loud enough to be heard by all employees in the facility, and the warning announcement should be preceded by a distinct signal to get the attention of the employees. Test the warning system frequently to make sure it is in working condition.

Don't forget about employees with disabilities, such as hearing loss. Establish some type of procedure that will alert such employees, e.g., a flashing bulb at or near their work station. In addition, a member of the emergency management team should be appointed to make sure disabled employees are located and given assistance in an emergency situation.

EVACUATION PLANNING

It is important to develop an evacuation policy and procedure in case it is necessary to leave the facility immediately, e.g., if there is a fire, bomb threat or toxic chemical spill.

Depending on the size of your facility and the number of employees, one or more members of the emergency management team should be responsible for assisting employees in the evacuation and accounting for personnel. Again, the needs of disabled employees should be considered, e.g., an evacuation route that can accommodate an employee in a wheelchair. In addition, emergency management team members who assist in the evacuation must be trained to recognize when they should evacuate the facility for their own safety.

Evacuation routes should be clearly marked with direction signs and the route should be well lit. A backup generator should be used to operate the lights along the evacuation route in case there is a power outage. There should be a primary evacuation route and alternate routes in case the primary route is blocked or otherwise impassable, e.g., a fire is concentrated in the area of the primary evacuation route.

Designate a staging area where all personnel and visitors to your facility should meet following evacuation. Make sure employees know that they are to report to the designated area for accounting purposes instead of proceeding home. A method should be devised to identify visitors to your facility—e.g., mandatory sign in/sign out sheets—to facilitate an accurate accounting of visitors to your facility. All employees and other visitors to the facility must be accurately accounted for to avoid unnecessary and dangerous search and rescue missions.

High Rise Buildings

If your business is located in a "high-rise building," appropriate exits, alarms, emergency lighting, communication systems, and sprinkler systems are critical for employee safety. In addition, routes leading to the exits, as well as the areas beyond the exits, must be accessible and free from materials or items that would impede individuals from easily and effectively evacuating the building.

A high rise building is defined by the National Fire Protection Association as: "a building greater than 75 feet in height where the building is measured from the lowest of fire department vehicle access to the floor of the highest occupiable story." State and local building code officials will assist you in determining whether the design and safety systems in the high-rise building are adequate and conform to code requirements.

Insofar as it is difficult evacuating a high-rise building, it is critical to the safety of your employees to prepare and practice your evacuation plan. The plan should be posted prominently on each floor. Workers with special needs or disabilities should be identified and special plans should be devised to make sure they are assisted out of the building during the evacuation.

In addition, you should make sure that the fire exits are not locked, and the doorways, halls and stairways are not obstructed. Emergency backup systems, such as lighting and communication capabilities, should be tested regularly. Meeting areas should be designated outside of the building following the evacuation.

SHELTER

Some emergencies, such as a tornado, require immediate shelter, which may be located inside or outside the facility. Appropriate shelters should be identified. Emergency supplies, such as flashlights, food, water, first aid supplies, etc., should be kept in the shelter.

A list of recommended emergency supplies is set forth in Appendix 5.

EQUIPMENT AND DATA PROTECTION

An important component of disaster preparation is making sure all important documents, electronic files, and other data are safely stored, and equipment and inventory required for the operation of your business is protected.

Most businesses maintain business records and files that are essential to business operations on company premises. Many businesses also store their product inventory on-site. If there is a disaster, equipment damage and loss of essential records and inventory is likely, and can delay your return to normal business operations.

Determine the vulnerability of your essential files, and other materials and equipment, to different types of disasters, such as a fire, flood, hurricane, etc., and take steps to protect them. Depending on the nature of the emergency, if at all possible, measures should be put in place to protect the facility, the equipment and business records. This will enable the company to restore business operations quickly following an emergency.

Equipment Protection

Consider the location of any equipment that is susceptible to damage. Make sure your equipment is secure. The force of some disasters can damage or destroy important equipment. For example, equipment near a hot water tank or pipes could be damaged if the pipes burst during an earthquake, and equipment near large windows could be damaged during hurricanes.

There are equipment protection systems available that will detect abnormalities and will shut down equipment if a potential problem is detected, e.g., a lightning strike or flood. In addition, you should install fire extinguishers, smoke alarms, and detectors in appropriate places.

Conduct a room-by-room walk through to determine what equipment may need to be secured, such as equipment that could move or fall during an earthquake or tornado. You can attach equipment and cabinets to walls or other stable equipment for fortification. Move heavy and fragile objects to low shelves. If you are dealing with a flood, elevate your equipment off of the floor to avoid electrical hazards in the event of flooding. In particular, computers should be kept above the flood level and moved them away from large windows.

Maintain an Inventory

For both insurance and tax purposes, you should maintain written and photographic inventories of all important materials and equipment, including computers, copy machines, printers, fax machines, etc. Establish a file for all equipment-related information, including purchase receipts, warranty information, instruction manuals, etc.

Record the model numbers and serial numbers for each piece of equipment. This information will be needed in case your equipment is damaged and needs to be repaired or replaced. Estimate the cost of repairing or replacing each essential piece of equipment in your business. Your estimates will help you assess your vulnerability. Maintain a list of reliable vendors who can be called to repair your equipment if it is damaged. Your completed equipment inventory should be stored in a safety deposit box or other secure location

A sample computer inventory form is set forth in Appendix 6.

Data Protection and Storage

It is important to protect vital business records, which may include:

1. Financial information;

2. Billing and payroll information;

3. Customer lists;

4. Insurance documents;

5. Engineering plans;

6. Product lists;

7. Employee records;

8. Supplier and customer databases; and

9. Trade secrets and proprietary information.

Failing to back up and store data is an irresponsible business practice. If your business gathers a lot of information, you should back up data frequently. Regularly back up essential electronic files. This is one of the most effective ways to protect against data loss. Always verify that the backup was successful and the correct data was stored.

In the event of an electrical surge or lightning strike, an uninterruptible power supply (UPS) with a battery backup system will protect your computer from damage and keep your computer running in the event of a power outage, allowing you time to save your work and avoid potential data loss.

It is a good idea to store all of your backup files in a secure off-site location. If a disaster strikes, such as a fire or flood, and you are displaced from your regular place of business, you will still have access to your essential files and may be able to stay in business by using the off-site files in a temporary location. If you cannot store your files off-site, you should keep them in a waterproof, fireproof safe.

PUBLIC INFORMATION AND MEDIA RELATIONS

Depending on the nature of your business, an emergency at your facility, such as a toxic chemical spill or gas leakage, could impact public health and safety. Therefore, it is important to keep the public informed about:

1. The nature and extent of the incident;

2. Whether the public health and safety is in danger;

3. The steps your company is taking to resolve the problem; and

4. What measures your company will take to prevent another similar incident from occurring in the future.

During an emergency, the media are often the most important link to the public. Try to develop and maintain positive relations with media outlets in your area. Determine how you would communicate important public information through the media in an emergency. Designate a trained spokesperson to talk to the media. Make sure any information that is disseminated through the media is accurate and complete. Avoid speculation about the incident. Any such information should be approved by company management before it is released to the public. Keep a record of any information released to the public.

MEDICAL EMERGENCIES

You must prepare for medical emergencies. Encourage employees to take basic first aid and CPR training. Provide training and certification at your facility, if possible. You can check with your local American Red Cross chapter to see whether they offer such training. In addition, keep first aid supplies in stock and make sure all of the employees have easy access to the supplies.

The American Red Cross recommends that the following items should be kept in a workplace disaster kit:

First Aid Supplies

1. Adhesive bandages in various sizes, including sterile dressing; rolled gauze bandages; gauze pads; triangular bandages; and a roll of cohesive bandage.

2. Germicidal hand wipes or waterless alcohol-based hand sanitizer.

3. Antiseptic wipes.

4. Large medical grade non-latex gloves.

5. Adhesive tape (2" width).

6. Anti-bacterial ointment.

7. Cold pack.

8. Scissors.

9. Tweezers.

10. A CPR breathing barrier, such as a face shield.

Food

Food should be non-perishable, require no refrigeration, preparation or cooking, and little or no water. The following items are suggested:

1. Ready-to-eat canned meals, meats, fruits, and vegetables.
2. Canned juices.
3. High-energy foods, such as granola bars, energy bars, etc.

Water

Store water in plastic containers such as soft drink bottles. Avoid using containers that will decompose or break, such as milk cartons or glass bottles.

Medications

Include usual non-prescription medications including pain relievers, stomach remedies, etc. Any employee who uses prescription medications should keep at least a three-day supply of these medications at the workplace.

Miscellaneous Items

1. Flashlights - Use flashlight to get around if the power is out. Do not use candles or any other open flame for emergency lighting.
2. Battery - powered radios-News about the emergency may change rapidly as events unfold. Radio reports will give information about the areas most affected.
3. Emergency blankets.
4. Paper plates and cups, and plastic utensils.
5. A non-electric can opener.
6. Personal hygiene items including bathroom tissue, toothbrushes, toothpaste, combs, brushes, soap, contact lens supplies, and feminine supplies, etc.
7. Plastic garbage bags and ties for personal sanitation uses.
8. Each employee should keep at least one complete change of clothing and footwear, including a long sleeved shirt and long pants, as well as closed-toed shoes or boots, at the workplace.
9. Employees who wear glasses should keep an extra pair at the workplace.

EMERGENCY MANAGEMENT COSTS

The cost of developing and implementing an emergency management plan depends on the size and nature of your business. Many of the emergency planning recommendations can be undertaken at little or no cost. For example, it doesn't cost anything to: (1) meet with your insurance provider to review coverage; (2) form an emergency management team; (3) create an evacuation and shelter plan; (4) create an emergency contact list; (5) conduct emergency drills, etc.

There is some expense involved in purchasing emergency equipment and supplies, however, the amounts are not cost prohibitive for most small businesses, e.g., purchasing a fire extinguisher, smoke alarm, first aid kit, portable safe, and creating backup computer files, etc.

More costlier items may include: (1) purchasing additional insurance; (2) purchasing and installing backup generators; (3) installing automatic sprinkler systems; and (4) upgrading the heating and air conditioning systems to filtrate air, etc.

Disaster planning is essential in order to protect the lives and well-being of your employees and customers, as well as your business investment. The cost of putting together a basic emergency management plan is comparatively negligible and well worth the expense.

EMPLOYEES AND THEIR FAMILIES

In an emergency, your employees will need to know whether their families are okay. Consider ways to help employees prepare their families for emergencies. This will increase their personal safety and help your business get back up and running. Those who are prepared at home will be better able to carry out their responsibilities at work.

Also, encourage employees to consider how they would communicate with their families in case they are separated from one another or injured in an emergency. Employees should arrange for an out-of-town contact for all family members to call in case of an emergency, and designate a place to meet family members in case they cannot get home in an emergency. If your employees and their families are prepared, your company is in a better position in an emergency situation.

CHAPTER 3:
PLANNING FOR SPECIFIC DISASTERS

IN GENERAL

This chapter sets forth planning considerations for many different types of disaster scenarios. Obviously, if your business is located in Florida, you won't be planning for a severe winter storm. You should tailor your emergency management plan to include those hazards that pose the greatest danger to your business.

Be aware, however, that you must be able to respond to an emergency in your community that could affect your business operations, even if your business is not itself vulnerable to a certain hazard. For example, you may be located near a facility that uses hazardous materials. A toxic spill at that facility will necessarily affect your business operations, and may necessitate an evacuation of your facility, or require some other response for which your business should also be prepared.

FIRES

Fire is the most common of all disasters. Every year fires cause thousands of deaths and injuries and billions of dollars in property damage. It is important that your company pays careful attention to fire safety to avoid such a tragedy.

Planning Considerations – Fires

When developing your emergency management plan, consider the following FEMA recommendations concerning fires:

1. Meet with the fire department to discuss the community's fire response capabilities. Talk about your operations. Identify processes and materials that could cause or fuel a fire, or contaminate the environment in a fire.

2. Have your facility inspected for fire hazards. Ask about fire codes and regulations.

3. Ask your insurance carrier to recommend fire prevention and protection measures. Your carrier may also offer training.

4. Distribute fire safety information to employees, including information on how to: (a) prevent fires in the workplace; (b) contain a fire; (c) evacuate the facility; and (d) where to report a fire.

5. Instruct personnel to use the stairs—not the elevators—in a fire. Also, instruct them to crawl on their hands and knees when escaping a hot or smoke-filled area.

6. Conduct evacuation drills. Post maps of evacuation routes in prominent places. Keep evacuation routes, including stairways and doorways, clear of debris.

7. Assign fire wardens for each area to monitor shutdown and evacuation procedures.

8. Establish procedures for the safe handling and storage of flammable liquids and gases.

9. Establish procedures to prevent the accumulation of combustible materials.

10. Provide for the safe disposal of smoking materials.

11. Establish a preventive maintenance schedule to keep equipment operating safely.

12. Place fire extinguishers in appropriate locations.

13. Train employees in the use of fire extinguishers.

14. Install smoke detectors. Check the smoke detectors once a month, and change the batteries at least once a year.

15. Establish a system for warning personnel of a fire. Consider installing a fire alarm with automatic notification to the fire department.

16. Consider installing a sprinkler system, fire hoses and fire-resistant walls and doors.

17. Ensure that key personnel are familiar with all fire safety systems.

18. Identify and mark all utility shutoffs so that electrical power, gas, or water can be shut off quickly by fire wardens or responding personnel.

19. Determine the level of response your facility will take if a fire occurs. Among the options are:

    (a) Option 1 - Immediate evacuation of all personnel on alarm.

    (b) Option 2 - All personnel are trained in fire extinguisher use. Personnel in the immediate area of a fire attempt to control it. If they cannot, the fire alarm is sounded and all personnel evacuate.

    (c) Option 3 - Only designated personnel are trained in fire extinguisher use.

    (d) Option 4 - A fire team is trained to fight incipient-stage fires that can be controlled without protective equipment or breathing apparatus. Beyond this level fire, the team evacuates.

    (e) Option 5 - A fire team is trained and equipped to fight structural fires using protective equipment and breathing apparatus.

HAZARDOUS MATERIALS

Hazardous materials are substances that are either flammable or combustible, explosive, toxic, noxious, corrosive, oxidizable, an irritant or radioactive. A hazardous material spill or release can pose a risk to life, health or property. An incident can result in the evacuation of a few people, a section of a facility or an entire neighborhood.

The Occupational Safety and Health Administration (OSHA) publishes a list of toxic and reactive highly hazardous chemicals which present the potential for a catastrophic event at certain threshold levels.

The OSHA list of hazardous chemicals is set forth in Appendix 7.

Hazardous Materials Regulation

There are a number of Federal laws that regulate hazardous materials, including: (1) The Superfund Amendments and Reauthorization Act of 1986 (SARA); (2) The Resource Conservation and Recovery Act of 1976 (RCRA); (3) The Hazardous Materials Transportation Act (HMTA); (4) The Occupational Safety and Health Act (OSHA); (5) The Toxic Substances Control Act (TSCA); and (6) The Clean Air Act.

Title III of SARA regulates the packaging, labeling, handling, storage and transportation of hazardous materials. The law requires businesses to furnish information about the quantities and health effects of materials used at their facility, and to promptly notify local and State officials whenever a significant release of hazardous materials occurs.

Planning Considerations – Hazardous Materials

When developing your emergency management plan, consider the following FEMA recommendations concerning hazardous materials:

1. Identify and label all hazardous materials stored, handled, produced and disposed of by your facility. Follow government regulations that apply to your facility. Obtain material safety data sheets for all hazardous materials at your location.

2. Ask the local fire department for assistance in developing appropriate response procedures.

3. Train employees to recognize and report hazardous material spills and releases. Train employees in proper handling and storage.

4. Establish a hazardous material response plan.

5. Establish procedures to notify management and emergency response organizations of an incident.

6. Establish procedures to warn employees of an incident.

7. Establish evacuation procedures.

8. Depending on your business operations, organize and train an emergency response team to confine and control hazardous material spills in accordance with applicable regulations.

9. Identify other businesses in your area that use hazardous materials. Determine whether an incident at another facility could affect your facility.

10. Identify highways, railroads and waterways near your facility used for the transportation of hazardous materials. Determine how a transportation accident near your facility could affect your operations.

Off-Site Incidents

As discussed above, you should be aware of the potential for an off-site hazardous materials incident that may affect your business operations. In such a case, evacuation may not be the preferable course of action. If hazardous materials—chemical, biological or radiological contaminants—have been accidentally or intentionally released into the atmosphere, authorities may advise you to have your employees "shelter-in-place." Because information will most likely be provided on television and radio, it is important to have a television or radio kept on during the workday in some area of your facility.

Shelter-in-place is a precaution aimed to keep you safe while remaining indoors. This is not the same thing as going to a shelter in case of a storm. Shelter-in-place means selecting a small, interior room, with no or few windows, and taking refuge there. It does not mean sealing off your entire office building.

If your business is advised by authorities to shelter-in-place, you should take the following steps:

1. Close the business.

2. If there are customers, clients, or visitors in the building, provide for their safety by asking them to stay–not leave the building. Nobody should attempt to drive or walk outdoors.

3. Unless there is an imminent threat, ask employees, customers, clients, and visitors to call their emergency contact to let them know where they are and that they are safe.

4. Turn on call-forwarding or alternative telephone answering systems or services. If the business has voice mail or an automated attendant, change the recording to indicate that the business is closed, and that staff and visitors are remaining in the building until authorities advise it is safe to leave.

5. Close and lock all windows, exterior doors, and any other openings to the outside.

6. If you are told there is danger of explosion, close the window shades, blinds, or curtains.

7. Have employees familiar with your building's mechanical systems turn off all fans, heating systems, and air conditioning systems. Some systems automatically provide for exchange of inside air with outside air. Such systems, in particular, need to be turned off, sealed, or disabled.

8. Gather essential disaster supplies, such as nonperishable food, bottled water, battery-powered radios, first aid supplies, flashlights, batteries, duct tape, plastic sheeting, and plastic garbage bags.

9. Select interior room(s) above the ground floor, with the fewest windows or vents. The room(s) should have adequate space for everyone to be able to sit in. Avoid overcrowding by selecting several rooms if necessary. Large storage closets, utility rooms, pantries, copy and conference rooms without exterior windows will work well. Avoid selecting a room with mechanical equipment like ventilation blowers or pipes, because this equipment may not be able to be sealed from the outdoors.

10. It is ideal to have a hard-wired telephone in the room you select. Call emergency contacts and have the phone available if you need to report a life-threatening condition. Cellular telephone equipment may be overwhelmed or damaged during an emergency.

11. Use duct tape and heavy plastic sheeting to seal all cracks around the door and any vents into the room.

12. Bring everyone into the room and shut and lock the door.

13. Write down the names of everyone in the room, and call your designated emergency contact to report who is in the room with you, and their affiliation with your business, e.g., employee, visitor, client, customer, etc.

14. Listen to the radio or television until you are told all is safe or you are told to evacuate. Local officials may call for evacuation in specific areas at greatest risk in your community.

FLOODS

Floods are the most common and widespread of all natural disasters. Most communities in the United States experience some degree of flooding after spring rains, heavy thunderstorms or winter snow thaws. Most floods develop slowly over a period of days. Flash floods, however, are like walls of water that develop in a matter of minutes. Flash floods can be caused by intense storms or dam failure, as demonstrated by the flooding catastrophe caused by Hurricane Katrina.

Planning Considerations – Floods

When developing your emergency management plan, consider the following FEMA recommendations concerning floods:

1. Determine your risk by asking your local emergency management office whether your facility is located in a flood plain. Learn the history of flooding in your area. Learn the elevation of your facility in relation to streams, rivers and dams.

2. Review the community's emergency plan. Learn the community's evacuation routes. Know where to find higher ground in case of a flood.

3. Establish warning and evacuation procedures for the facility. Make plans for assisting employees who may need transportation.

4. Inspect areas in your facility subject to flooding. Identify records and equipment that can be moved to a higher location. Make plans to move records and equipment in case of flood.

5. Purchase a National Oceanic and Atmospheric Administration (NOAA) Weather Radio with a warning alarm tone and battery backup. Listen for flood watches and warnings:

   (a) Flood Watch – A flood watch indicates that flooding is possible.

   (b) Flood Warning – A flood warning indicates that flooding is already occurring or will occur soon.

6. Ask your insurance carrier for information about flood insurance. Regular property and casualty insurance does not cover flooding.

7. Consider the feasibility of flood-proofing your facility.

HURRICANES

Hurricanes are severe tropical storms with sustained winds of 74 miles per hour or greater. Hurricane winds can reach 160 miles per hour and extend inland for hundreds of miles. Hurricanes bring torrential rains and produce a storm surge of ocean water that crashes into land as the storm approaches. Tornadoes can also be spawned by hurricanes. Hurricane advisories are issued by the National Weather Service as soon as a hurricane appears to be a threat. The hurricane season lasts from June through November.

Planning Considerations – Hurricanes

When developing your emergency management plan, consider the following FEMA recommendations concerning hurricanes:

1. Ask your local emergency management office about community evacuation plans.

2. Establish facility shutdown procedures.

3. Establish warning and evacuation procedures.

4. Make plans for assisting employees who may need transportation.

5. Make plans for communicating with employees' families before and after a hurricane.

6. Purchase a National Oceanic and Atmospheric Administration (NOAA) Weather Radio with a warning alarm tone and battery backup. Listen for hurricane watches and warnings:

   (a) Hurricane Watch – A hurricane watch indicates that a hurricane is possible within 24 to 36 hours.

   Hurricane Warning - A hurricane warning indicates that a hurricane will hit land within 24 hours.

7. Survey your facility. Make plans to protect outside equipment and structures.

8. Make plans to protect windows. Permanent storm shutters offer the best protection. Covering windows with 5/8' marine plywood is a second option.

9. Consider the need for backup systems, including:

    (a) Portable pumps to remove flood water;

    (b) Alternate power sources such as generators or gasoline-powered pumps; and

    (c) Battery-powered emergency lighting.

10. Prepare to move records, computers and other items within your facility or to another location, if necessary.

TORNADOES

Tornadoes are incredibly violent local storms that extend to the ground with whirling winds that can reach 300 mph. Tornadoes can uproot trees and buildings and turn harmless objects into deadly missiles in a matter of seconds. The path of damage caused by a tornado can exceed one mile wide and 50 miles long. Tornadoes can take place in any state, but occur more frequently in the Midwest, Southeast and Southwest, oftentimes with little or no warning.

Planning Considerations – Tornadoes

When developing your emergency management plan, consider the following FEMA recommendations concerning tornadoes:

1. Ask your local emergency management office about the community's tornado warning system.

2. Purchase a National Oceanic and Atmospheric Administration (NOAA) Weather Radio with a warning alarm tone and battery backup. Listen for tornado watches and warnings:

    (a) Tornado Watch – A tornado watch indicates that a tornado is likely.

    (b) Tornado Warning - A tornado warning indicates that a tornado has been sighted in the area or is indicated by radar.

3. Establish procedures to inform employees when tornado warnings are posted. Consider the need for spotters to be responsible for looking out for approaching storms.

4. Work with a structural engineer or architect to designate shelter areas in your facility. Ask your local emergency management office or National Weather Service office for guidance.

5. Consider the amount of space you will need.

6. The best protection in a tornado is usually an underground area. If an underground area is not available, consider:

   (a) Small interior rooms on the lowest floor and without windows, such as a break room or conference room;

   (b) Hallways on the lowest floor away from doors and windows; and

   (c) Rooms constructed with reinforced concrete, brick or block with no windows and a heavy concrete floor or roof system overhead.

7. Make plans for evacuating personnel away from lightweight modular offices, as these structures offer no protection from tornadoes.

8. Conduct tornado drills.

9. Once in the shelter, employees should protect their heads with their arms and crouch down.

SEVERE WINTER STORMS

Severe winter storms bring heavy snow, ice, strong winds and freezing rain. Winter storms can prevent employees and customers from reaching the facility, leading to a temporary shutdown until roads are cleared. Heavy snow and ice can also cause structural damage and power outages.

Planning Considerations – Severe Winter Storms

When developing your emergency management plan, consider the following FEMA recommendations concerning severe winter storms:

1. Listen to a National Oceanic and Atmospheric Administration (NOAA) Weather Radio and local radio and television stations for weather information. Listen for winter storm watches and warnings:

   (a) Winter Storm Watch – A winter storm watch indicates that severe winter weather is possible.

   (b) Winter Storm Warning – A winter storm warning indicates that severe winter weather is expected.

   (c) Blizzard Warning – A blizzard warning indicates that severe winter weather with sustained winds of at least 35 mph is expected.

   (d) Traveler's Advisory – A traveler's advisory indicates that severe winter conditions may make driving difficult or dangerous.

2. Establish procedures for facility shutdown and early release of your employees.

3. Store food, water, blankets, battery-powered radios with extra batteries and other emergency supplies for employees who become stranded at the facility.

4. Provide a backup power source for critical operations.

5. Arrange for snow and ice removal from parking lots, walkways, loading docks, etc.

EARTHQUAKES

An earthquake is a sudden, rapid shaking of the Earth caused by the breaking and shifting of rock beneath the Earth's surface. There are 45 states and territories in the United States at moderate to very high risk from earthquakes, and they are located in every region of the country. California experiences the most frequent damaging earthquakes. Earthquakes strike suddenly, without warning. Earthquakes can occur at any time of the year and at any time of the day or night. On a yearly basis, 70 to 75 damaging earthquakes occur throughout the world.

Earthquakes can seriously damage buildings and their contents; disrupt gas, electric and telephone services; and trigger landslides, avalanches, flash floods, fires and huge ocean waves called tsunamis. Aftershocks can occur for weeks following an earthquake. In many buildings, the greatest danger to people in an earthquake is when equipment and non-structural elements such as ceilings, partitions, windows and lighting fixtures shake loose.

In January 1994, an earthquake struck Northridge, California, a modern urban community generally designed to withstand the forces of earthquakes. Its economic cost has been estimated at $20 billion, with relatively few lives lost. One year later, Kobe, Japan, a densely populated community which is less prepared for earthquakes than Northridge, was devastated by the most costly earthquake ever to occur. Property losses were projected at $96 billion, and at least 5,378 people were killed. These two earthquakes tested building codes and construction practices, as well as emergency preparedness and response procedures.

Planning Considerations – Earthquakes

When developing your emergency management plan, consider the following FEMA recommendations concerning earthquakes:

1. Assess your facility's vulnerability to earthquakes. Ask local government agencies for seismic information for your area.

2. Have your facility inspected by a structural engineer. Develop and prioritize strengthening measures, if necessary.

3. Follow safety codes when constructing a facility or making major renovations.

4. Inspect non-structural systems such as air conditioning, communications and pollution control systems. Assess the potential for damage. Prioritize measures to prevent damages.

5. Inspect your facility for any item that could fall, spill, break or move during an earthquake and take steps to reduce these hazards, e.g., by moving large and heavy objects to lower shelves or on the floor, and securing furniture and other equipment, etc.

6. Keep copies of design drawings of the facility to be used in assessing the facility's safety after an earthquake.

7. Review processes for handling and storing hazardous materials. Have incompatible chemicals stored separately.

8. Ask your insurance carrier about earthquake insurance and mitigation techniques.

9. Establish procedures to determine whether an evacuation is necessary after an earthquake.

10. Designate areas in the facility away from exterior walls and windows where employees and visitors should gather after an earthquake if an evacuation is not necessary.

11. Conduct earthquake drills. Provide employees with the following safety information:

    (a) If you are indoors when an earthquake strikes, stay inside and take cover under a sturdy piece of furniture or counter, or brace yourself against an inside wall. Protect your head and neck.

    (b) If you are outdoors when an earthquake strikes, move into the open, away from buildings, street lights and utility wires.

    (c) After an earthquake, stay away from windows, skylights and items that could fall, and do not use the elevators.

    (d) Use stairways to leave the building if it is determined that a building evacuation is necessary.

TECHNOLOGICAL EMERGENCIES

Technological emergencies include any interruption or loss of a utility service, power source, life support system, information system or equipment needed to keep the business in operation.

Planning Considerations – Technological Emergencies

When developing your emergency management plan, consider the following FEMA recommendations concerning technological emergencies:

1. Identify all critical operations, including:

    (a) Utilities including electric power, gas, water, hydraulics, compressed air, municipal and internal sewer systems, wastewater treatment services.

    (b) Security and alarm systems, elevators, lighting, life support systems, heating, ventilation and air conditioning systems, electrical distribution system.

    (c) Manufacturing equipment, pollution control equipment.

    (d) Communication systems, both data and voice computer networks.

    (e) Transportation systems including air, highway, railroad and waterway.

2. Determine the impact of service disruption.

3. Ensure that key safety and maintenance personnel are thoroughly familiar with all building systems.

4. Establish procedures for restoring systems.

5. Determine the need for backup systems.

6. Establish preventive maintenance schedules for all systems and equipment.

CHAPTER 4:
PREPARING YOUR WORKPLACE
FOR A PANDEMIC

WHAT IS A PANDEMIC?

A pandemic is a global disease outbreak. An influenza pandemic occurs when a new influenza virus emerges for which there is little or no immunity in the human population. Due to the lack of immunity, the virus spreads easily from person to person. Pandemics can vary in severity. A particularly severe influenza pandemic can result in a worldwide catastrophe, causing widespread illness and deaths. Thus, planning for a pandemic influenza is essential to minimize a pandemic's impact.

An influenza pandemic differs from what is known as the "flu season" in the United States. Seasonal influenza is the periodic outbreak of a respiratory illness that occurs in the fall and winter months. Most people have some immunity to the particular strain of virus, and a vaccine is generally prepared in advance of the season for those who may be at risk for complications from the illness, such as the elderly and young children.

Influenza is spread primarily through large droplets that contact a person's nose, mouth or eyes when an infected person coughs, sneezes or talks. Generally, these droplets have a limited range of no more than 6 feet, thus close contact with an infected person should be avoided. Influenza may also be spread by touching contaminated objects, and then touching one's nose, mouth or eyes.

Currently, there is no influenza pandemic, however, many scientists believe it is only a matter of time before a pandemic occurs. Pandemics have occurred throughout history, and it is impossible to predict when the next one will occur, and whether it will be mild or severe.

There has been much concern recently over Avian influenza, commonly referred to as "bird flu" because it is caused by a virus that infects wild birds and domestic poultry. Of particular concern is the H5N1 strain of avian influenza because it is one of the deadliest viruses known to have crossed the species barrier between birds and humans.

Most human cases of the virus have resulted from contact with infected poultry, and the spread of the virus from person to person has been limited to rare cases. However, because there is no human immunity to this virus, if widespread transmission from person to person was to occur, a deadly pandemic could result over a relatively short period of time.

EFFECT OF A PANDEMIC ON BUSINESS OPERATIONS

Unlike a natural disaster, or even a terrorist event, an influenza pandemic will simultaneously affect many regions in this country, as well as other countries. Outbreaks could continue to occur for a year or more. During a pandemic, your business would likely experience the following setbacks:

1. Absenteeism - A pandemic could affect as many as 40 percent of the workforce during periods of peak influenza illness. Employees could be absent because they are sick or must care for sick family members. In addition, employees may be afraid to leave their home and come to work during an outbreak.

2. Decrease in Commerce - During a pandemic, consumer demand for goods—other than those items related to infection control—may decline. In addition, consumers may be less likely to leave their home to shop in crowded stores, preferring to shop online or in other ways that reduce person-to-person contact.

3. Delivery Interruption – Shipment of goods from areas that are severely affected by the pandemic may be delayed or cancelled.

ROLE OF THE EMPLOYER

In the event of an influenza pandemic, employers will play a key role in protecting the health and safety of employees, and helping to limit the impact on the economy. To reduce the impact of a pandemic on your business operations, as well as your employees and customers, it is important to plan ahead. Proper planning will allow employers to better protect their employees and prepare for changing patterns of commerce and potential disruptions in supplies or services.

LEVEL OF RISK

The level of risk of occupational exposure to influenza during a pandemic depends on whether employees work in close proximity to persons who are potentially infected with the virus, or whether it is a requirement of the job to have repeated or extended contact with persons known to be infected.

High risk occupations include those with high potential for exposure to known or suspected sources of infection, such as persons who work in laboratories dealing with the influenza virus. Medium risk occupations include those that require frequent, close contact with known or suspected sources of infection, such as schoolteachers, nurses, etc. And, low risk occupations include those that do not require contact with known or suspected sources of infection or the general public. The vast majority of workplaces are likely to be in the medium or low exposure risk groups Nevertheless, even at the lower risk levels, employers must err on the side of caution and develop a plan to minimize the spread of infection in the workplace.

PLANNING CONSIDERATIONS

As with any emergency, being prepared is key to surviving any disaster. Include pandemic preparedness in your emergency management plan and consider the recommendations listed below when preparing for a pandemic.

A checklist for pandemic planning is set forth in Appendix 8.

Community Planning

It is important to work with community planners to integrate your pandemic plan into local and state planning. This will allow you to access resources and information promptly to maintain business operations and keep your employees safe.

Review Your Emergency Plan Regularly

Review and update your emergency management plan regularly and conduct drills to make sure the plan is workable. Review pandemic influenza plans available from federal, state and local health departments and incorporate actions you deem appropriate for your workplace.

Designate an employee, a website, a bulletin board or other means of communicating important pandemic flu information. Use signs to keep customers informed about symptoms of influenza.

Contingency Planning

Plan to run your business with a reduced workforce. Cross-train employees so that they are able to cover for absent employees who have critical positions with the company in case of a pandemic. Provide training, education and informational material about business-essential job functions.

Develop an emergency sick leave policy that deters infected employees from coming to work. Penalizing a sick worker for staying home will result in the infected employee showing up at the workplace and likely infecting more employees, further reducing the workforce.

Identify and Minimize Risks

Identify possible exposure and health risks to your employees. Develop practices that place distance between employees, customers and the general public. Use methods of doing business that minimize personal contact, such as email and teleconferencing. If possible, arrange for employees to work from their home during an outbreak.

Keep work surfaces, telephones, computer equipment and other frequently touched surfaces and office equipment clean. Discourage your employees from using other employees' phones, desks, offices or other work tools and equipment

All employers should implement good hygiene and infection control practices. Stockpile infection control supplies including soap, tissue, hand sanitizer, cleaning supplies and recommended personal protective equipment, such as gloves or surgical masks. Provide your employees and customers with easy access to these infection control supplies.

Emergency supplies should include a first aid kit; dust or filter masks; sanitary towelettes; tools; plastic sheeting and duct tape to seal off areas; a battery-powered commercial radio; extra batteries; flashlights; water; and food.

Individual employees should maintain a personal safety kit that includes everything the individual may require to meet their personal needs, including essential medications.

Assist Employees in Crisis

Work with your insurance companies, and state and local health agencies to provide information to employees and customers about medical care in the event of a pandemic.

Provide opportunities for support, counseling, and mental health assessment and referral should these be necessary for employees who are experiencing grief due to loss of family, friends or co-workers, stress over personal and family illness, and fear for health and safety of friends and family.

EMPLOYEES WHO TRAVEL OUTSIDE THE UNITED STATES

Employees who travel out of the United States for work should be aware that other countries have different influenza seasons and would likely be affected by a pandemic at times different from the United States.

According to the U.S. Department of State, in the event of a pandemic, its ability to assist Americans traveling abroad may be severely limited by restrictions on local and international movement imposed for public health reasons, either by foreign governments and/or the United States.

Furthermore, the Department of State will not provide Americans travelling abroad with medications or supplies even in the event of a pandemic. American Embassy medical supplies cannot be made available to private American citizens abroad, therefore, employers and employees are encouraged to prepare appropriately

CHAPTER 5:
BUSINESS INSURANCE

IN GENERAL

Whether you own a home-based business, a small business, or a large-scale business with many employees, it is important to have some type of business insurance policy. You should not gamble when you've invested so much time and effort in your company. A disaster, such as a fire, flood or other event can completely wipe out everything you have worked so hard to build.

Maintaining adequate insurance can mean the difference between resuming business operations following a disaster, or closing down your business. Thus, it is very important to make sure your insurance policy is up-to-date and covers you for any losses that may be sustained if your business experiences a catastrophic event. In addition, make sure your policy is tailored to cover any specific needs of your company. For example, if your facility is located in a flood zone, make sure you have flood coverage.

It is best to make an appointment with your insurance representative to go over your existing business policy. Discuss all of the possible scenarios that could arise, and make sure your policy provides adequate coverage. A qualified insurance professional will be able to recommend coverage options that will help you evaluate the kind of protection and level of insurance coverage your business needs.

When purchasing a policy, or increasing coverage, you shouldn't get needless coverage; however, you don't want to overlook any risks that could cause you a significant loss. If a certain risk is remote but possible, the premium will probably be low and worth the extra money.

Unfortunately, it is only after a disaster has occurred that many businesses discover they are not adequately insured. This can be financially devastating and mean the difference between reopening or closing your business. Thus, it is important to discuss the following topics with your insurance agent to determine the needs of your business:

1. How your property will be valued.
2. Whether your policy covers the cost of required upgrades to code.
3. The perils or causes of loss covered by your policy.
4. The deductibles contained in your policy.
5. Your responsibilities in the event of a loss.
6. The types of records and documentation the insurance carrier will need in the event of a loss.
7. Whether your policy covers losses caused by an interruption of power.
8. Whether your policy covers lost income in the event of business interruption caused by a loss, and the amount and duration of such coverage.
9. Whether your policy covers reduced income due to a loss of customers when the business reopens.
10. Whether the development of an emergency management plan will reduce your rates.

An Insurance Coverage Discussion Form is set forth in Appendix 9.

BUSINESS OWNERS POLICY

Small and medium sized businesses that meet certain criteria are eligible to purchase an insurance package known as a business owners policy (BOP). Eligibility depends on certain criteria, such as the type of business, the size of the business premises, and the required liability limits. The cost of the policy is also based on the these factors, as well as the financial stability of the business, the construction of the facility, the availability of security features, the presence of risk factors, and the location of the business.

A business owners policy offers a combination of coverages including: (1) property insurance; (2) business interruption insurance; and (3) liability protection. Business owners policies do not cover professional liability, automobile insurance, workers' compensation or medical insurance, which would be covered under separate policies.

As discussed below, in the event of a disaster, the provisions of your property insurance and business interruption insurance policies will dictate how quickly your business can recover and resume operations.

PROPERTY INSURANCE

Property insurance covers the building owned by the company, and the contents of the building. Therefore, it is important for insurance purposes to take an inventory of all of your business property, and determine how much the property is worth, so you know how much insurance to purchase. You can always increase your coverage as your business grows and you acquire more property and additional equipment.

In addition, if your facility is completely destroyed in a fire or tornado, it would be very difficult to recall every piece of property owned by your business. If you maintain an up-to-date inventory, it will be easier for the insurance claims representative to verify your losses and settle your insurance claim, enabling you to get back to business as soon as possible.

A properly maintained inventory should include a list of all of the business property you own, including equipment, furnishings, product inventory, etc. Each item should be described in detail, and should include the make, model and serial number, vendor name and address, and the date of purchase. You should take photographs of large-ticket items. The list should be kept in a file along with any other documentation, such as the purchase receipt, sales contract, warranty information, instruction booklet, appraisal, etc.

Exclusions

In general, property insurance does not ordinarily cover floods, earthquakes and acts of terrorism. As set forth below, if your business is located in a flood or earthquake zone, you will have to purchase additional coverage.

Flood Coverage

Coverage for flood damage is generally excluded in most property insurance policies. Contact your local government office to find out whether your business is located in a flood zone. In high risk flood areas, coverage is mandatory for all properties receiving Federal or federally based assistance. The amount of flood insurance coverage required by the Flood Disaster Protection Act of 1973, as amended by the National Flood Insurance Reform Act of 1994, is the lesser of the following:

1. The maximum amount of National Flood Insurance Program (NFIP) coverage available for the particular property type;

2. The outstanding principal balance of the loan; or

3. The insurable value of the structure.

If the property is not in a high-risk area, but instead in a low to moderate-risk area, the law does not require flood insurance; however, it is recommended since historically about twenty-five percent of all flood claims come from such areas.

If you need flood insurance, contact your insurance agent or the National Flood Insurance Program (Telephone: 1-888-CALL-FLOOD/ Website: www.fema.gov/nfip/).

In addition, the federal government requires buildings in flood zones that don't conform to flood plain building codes to be torn down if damage exceeds 50 percent of the market value. If your facility is located in a flood zone, consider purchasing "ordinance or law" coverage to help pay for the extra costs of tearing down the structure and rebuilding it. Ordinance or Law policies cover the cost of rebuilding or repairing a building to comply with the most recent local building codes.

If you own a home business, you may need two flood insurance policies, a home policy and a separate business policy, depending on the percentage of the total square footage of your house that is devoted to business use. Check with your insurance agent if you have questions about your flood insurance provisions.

Earthquake Coverage

Coverage for earthquake damage is also excluded in most property insurance policies. If your facility is located in an earthquake-prone area, you will need to purchase a special earthquake insurance policy. In general, earthquake policies have a different kind of deductible, which is based on a percentage of coverage rather than a monetary figure. For example, if your facility were insured for $300,000 with a 5% deductible, you would be responsible for paying the first $15,000 in damage due to the earthquake.

Acts of Terrorism

Before the tragic events of September 11, 2001, standard commercial insurance policies included terrorism coverage as part of the package without additional cost. Today, terrorism coverage is generally offered separately at a price that more adequately reflects the current risk. Under the Terrorism Risk Insurance Act of 2002 (TRIA), only businesses that purchase optional terrorism coverage are covered for losses arising from terrorist acts. The TRIA was designed to enable commercial insurers to provide affordable terrorism coverage to policyholders. In 2005, President Bush signed the Terrorism Risk Insurance Extension Act of 2005, which extends the terms of the TRIA through December 31, 2007.

The TRIA establishes a program within the U.S. Treasury Department, under which the Federal government shares the risk of loss from future foreign terrorist attacks. If an act, certified to be a foreign act of terrorism, causes losses in excess of $5 million, participating insurers must pay a certain amount in claims—the deductible—before Federal assistance becomes available. For losses above the deductible, the government covers 90%, while the insurer contributes 10%. Losses covered by the program are capped at $100 billion, and the program permits the government to recoup the amounts paid by virtue of a surcharge on all policyholders.

All insurers who provide property or casualty insurance are required to participate in the program. The TRIA does not set forth pricing guidelines; however, states can invalidate any rates determined to be excessive, inadequate or unfairly discriminatory.

The Act applies only to foreign acts of terrorism, resulting in covered property damage within the United States. The TRIA does not limit the liability of any government, organization, or person who participated, conspired, aids and abets or commits an act of terrorism. The TRIA provides a federal cause of action—generally governed by the substantive law of the state where the act of terrorism occurred—as the exclusive remedy for claims arising out of or resulting from a terrorism act.

When considering the purchase of terrorism insurance coverage, you should carefully review all of the policy terms, conditions and exclusions, to determine whether your company would benefit from terrorism coverage.

Selected provisions of the Terrorism Risk Insurance Act of 2002 and the Terrorism Risk Insurance Extension Act of 2005 are set forth in Appendix 10.

BUSINESS INTERRUPTION INSURANCE

Most business owners have property insurance to cover damages caused by certain events, ranging from small claims to catastrophic events. However, property insurance does not compensate a business for losses that occur if the business has to shut down for days, weeks or months. In order to cover those types of losses, you must purchase business interruption insurance—also referred to as business income coverage. As stated above, business interruption insurance is usually available as a package along with property insurance.

Business interruption insurance is vital to the survival of your company following a disaster or any event that causes your business to shut down for a period of time. If your facility is destroyed, e.g., in a fire, you will be unable to continue operating and suffer extensive losses. Business interruption insurance compensates you for lost income if your business premises are uninhabitable due to disaster-related damage.

Lost profits are based on the amount of money your company would have earned if the disaster had not occurred. Business interruption insurance also covers temporary relocation expenses, if necessary, and ongoing operating expenses that must be paid whether or not the business is operating, such as utilities and advertising costs. As with most insurance policies, the cost of coverage depends on the risk involved. For example, business interruption insurance coverage for a business located in a flood zone will likely be costlier than another business. In addition, the type of business would also factor into the cost of coverage.

Business interruption insurance only applies if the cause of the damage is covered under your business property insurance policy. For example, if your business is flooded, you can only receive compensation if the company's property insurance policy covered flood damage. If the cause of your business interruption is not covered under the company's property insurance policy, you cannot make a claim.

Depending on the nature of the disaster and the extent of damage your business sustained, it can take time for you to resume operations. Thus, your policy limits should be sufficient to cover a reasonable amount of time. Most business interruption policies contain a 48-hour waiting period before coverage begins.

There are two types of business income interruption policies: (1) named perils policy; and (2) all-risk policy.

Named Perils Policy

A named perils policy covers risks that are specified in the policy, such as wind or fire damage. If the damage is caused by an event that is not named in the policy, the damage will not be covered. This type of policy may be suitable for business located in areas that are frequently subjected to certain types of disasters, such as floods or tornadoes. The cost of coverage will generally depend on the location of the business and the likelihood the specific event will occur.

All-Risk Policy

An all-risk policy covers damages caused by all types of perils except those specifically excluded. Risks typically excluded are flood and earthquake coverage; however, you can generally purchase coverage for these events for an additional premium. For example, flood insurance coverage is available under the National Flood Insurance Program discussed above. The advantage of this type of policy is that it covers you in the event of all types of disaster, even those you did not anticipate.

Extra Expense Insurance

Extra expense insurance coverage provides a business owner with funds above the company's normal operating expenses so the business does not have to shut down while it recovers from a catastrophic event. In some cases, extra expense coverage is sufficient without additional business interruption insurance.

FILING YOUR INSURANCE CLAIM

In order to file an insurance claim following a disaster, you should contact your insurance agent and insurance carrier as soon as possible. If you need to make immediate repairs to equipment to keep your business running, save the damaged parts and repair bills for the insurance adjuster.

If you need to repair or replace damaged property, obtain at least two bids from vendors. Keep detailed records of any expenses you incur in keeping your business operating.

If you need to make a business interruption claim, you will need to provide the insurance adjuster your financial records to demonstrate how much income your business generated before and after the event. For this reason, as discussed in Chapter 2 (Developing and Implementing the Emergency Plan), it is important to keep backup copies of important documents, such as financial records, in a safe place off of your business premises, in case a catastrophic event destroys your facility.

POLICY CANCELLATION

An insurance carrier is prohibited from cancelling an insurance policy that has been in force more than 60 days unless:

1. The insured fails to pay the required premium; and
2. The insured has committed fraud or has made a serious misrepresentation on the insurance application.

POLICY NONRENEWAL

When your insurance policy expires, both you and your insurance carrier can choose not to renew your insurance policy. Your insurance carrier must notify you within a certain period of time before the expiration date of its intention not to renew the policy, and must give you a reason why it will not renew your insurance coverage.

FILING A COMPLAINT AGAINST YOUR INSURANCE CARRIER

If your insurance representative is not handling the claim to your satisfaction, e.g.,—the offer of settlement does not adequately cover your losses—you should contact the complaint department of your insurance carrier. If this doesn't solve your problem, you can file your complaint with your state department of consumer affairs or state insurance department.

A directory of state insurance departments is set forth in Appendix 11.

As a last resort, you may have to consult a lawyer. Bring a copy of your insurance policy and any other relevant documents. Your attorney will intervene and try to resolve the problem you are having with the insurance carrier, e.g., obtain a better settlement on your behalf. If the insurance carrier is non-responsive, your attorney will determine whether you have a case worth taking to court.

CHAPTER 6:
DAMAGE ASSESSMENT AND RECOVERY

IN GENERAL

According to the U.S. Department of Labor, over 40% of businesses never reopen following a disaster. Of those businesses that do reopen, approximately 25% close within 2 years of the disaster. Small businesses, due to lack of available resources, are the most vulnerable after experiencing a catastrophic event. However, if you are determined to reopen, statistics show that companies that resume their business operations quickly have a better chance of survival.

DAMAGE ASSESSMENT

If you took the time to establish an emergency management plan for your business, as discussed in this Almanac, you will be better prepared to deal with the aftermath of a disaster and begin the rebuilding process. If you did not take proper precautions, you may still be able to recover from a disaster if you are diligent in your efforts, but it will take more time.

Before you can begin rebuilding following a disaster, you need to assess the nature and extent of physical damage your business has suffered, putting an emphasis on safety. If you own the building in which your company is located, you should have it inspected by a structural engineer before your employees and customers are permitted to enter the premises. If you do not own the building, make sure the owner has the building inspected. You are responsible for the safety of anyone on the premises whether or not you own the building.

If the building is not safe to enter, you must find an alternative location from which to operate your business. As further discussed in Chapter 5 (Business Insurance), you should call your insurance agent as soon as possible following the disaster to determine your coverage. For example, if you have business interruption insurance coverage, the cost of temporarily relocating your business operations may be covered under the policy. In addition, you must also consider the monetary losses your company will suffer while business operations are interrupted.

You should also make a list of all of the business property that has been destroyed or damaged, and estimate the replacement or repair costs. If you prepared an inventory list as discussed in Chapter 5 (Business Insurance), this task will be much easier. Without an inventory, it is likely you will not be able to recall all of the property you lost. Provide this information to your insurance adjuster.

Once it has been determined that your building is safe to re-enter, you need to form a recovery team to go inside and assess the damage. Photograph or videotape all of the damaged property. Make temporary repairs where possible to avoid additional damage, e.g., repair holes in the roof to prevent water damage from leaking ceilings. Remove debris and restore power. Protect undamaged property and secure the site. Restore your utilities, phone service, and gas lines, and if you discover a gas leak or live wire, contact your utility company immediately. Also, make sure your sprinkler system is in working order.

Separate damaged property from undamaged property. The insurance adjuster will want to view the damaged property so do not discard any of it. If you release any property to the adjuster, make sure you get a receipt stating the quantity and type of goods removed.

FINANCING YOUR RECOVERY

It is important to determine your financial position following a disaster. Does your property insurance policy adequately cover your losses? Did you purchase business interruption insurance to hold you over financially until your business is up and running again? Do you have enough money to rebuild and reopen your business? You must consider these questions in order to decide whether it makes sense to move forward with your recovery plans. If your business was in financial trouble before the disaster, recovery will be more difficult and less likely.

As discussed in Chapter 7 (The Small Business Administration Disaster Relief Loan Program), the Small Business Administration (SBA) offers affordable, timely and accessible financial help to businesses following a disaster through it's Office of Disaster Assistance. The SBA provides long-term, low-interest disaster loans to eligible businesses to cover both physical and economic injury.

In addition to SBA financial assistance, you may be eligible for help from the Internal Revenue Service to offset some of your disaster-related losses. For example, the IRS Code allows taxpayers to avoid recognizing gain when they receive insurance payments or other compensation for damaged or destroyed property if those payments are used to acquire new property. The IRS also initiated a series of public outreach efforts and worked with the American Institute of Certified Public Accountants (AICPA) and other groups to make sure that affected taxpayers are aware of the relief provisions available to them under the tax law. For more information, visit the IRS Web site [www.irs.gov].

Nevertheless, you cannot assume that your insurance policy will cover all of your losses, or that your business will be eligible for disaster loan assistance from the SBA. You must also consider other sources of financial aid, such as your savings, loans from family or friends, or personal lines of credit.

If you need advice on moving forward, one excellent resource for small business owners is SCORE "Counselors to America's Small Business," a non-profit volunteer small business counseling organization. SCORE's website provides several important links for small business owners affected by disaster.

You can contact SCORE as follows:

The SCORE Association

1175 Herndon Parkway, Suite 900

Herndon, VA 20170

Tel: 1-800-634-0245

Fax: 1-703-487-3066

Website: http://www.score.org/

GETTING BACK TO BUSINESS

As stated above, the sooner your business reopens following a disaster, the better its chances for survival. If a disaster has devastated a community, chances are your customers and suppliers have been affected as well. It is important to maintain contact with your customers and suppliers, and let them know you are resuming your business operations.

It is also important to maintain complete and accurate records to help ensure a more efficient recovery, such as customer lists, billing and payroll records, financial data, tax returns, and inventory control records, etc. If you implemented an emergency management plan, you should have backup records and data stored off-site. However, if you had no plan in place, chances are your records were destroyed. Although this may create more difficulties, you are not necessarily without recourse. For example, if you didn't keep backup copies of important financial papers, you may be able to recreate some or most of your files by contacting your accountant, bank or other financial institution and ask for copies.

ASSISTING YOUR EMPLOYEES

A large part of recovery involves your employees, who form the backbone of your business operations. It is important to demonstrate a caring attitude if you expect cooperation and productivity following a disaster. It is likely that your employees will need time to make sure their family members are okay, particularly if the disaster affected the entire community. If so, offer some paid leave time for employees to attend to family needs, if necessary.

It has been demonstrated that a workplace routine can help an individual recover by providing them with an opportunity to be more active. Thus, you should try and re-establish work routines as quickly as possible. Gather your employees together to discuss their needs. Encourage co-workers to talk openly with each other about their fears and hopes. If necessary, offer the services of professional counselors, at no charge, to help your employees address their fears and anxieties.

CHAPTER 7:
THE SMALL BUSINESS ADMINISTRATION DISASTER RELIEF LOAN PROGRAM

IN GENERAL

Following a disaster, one of the biggest needs a small business may have is the funds necessary to rebuild and resume business activities. Through its Office of Disaster Assistance (ODA), the Small Business Administration (SBA) provides affordable, timely and accessible financial assistance to businesses following a disaster. Disaster assistance has been part of the SBA's mission since its inception in 1953.

APPLYING FOR FINANCIAL ASSISTANCE

If your business is located in a declared disaster area and has suffered any disaster related damage, you may be eligible for federal disaster assistance. Businesses may apply directly to the Small Business Administration by submitting an SBA Disaster Loan application to:

The U.S. Small Business Administration

Processing and Disbursement Center

14925 Kingsport Rd.

Ft. Worth, TX 76155-2243

The SBA Loan Application is relatively simply to complete. SBA personnel are available to explain the forms and provide assistance in completing the necessary forms at no charge.

The application form basically requires the same information about the business and its substantial owners and managers that is generally required for a bank loan. In addition, personal guarantees by the principals of a business are required. In addition, the loan application requires:

1. An itemized list of losses with your estimate of the repair or replacement cost of each item;

2. A copy of certain federal income tax information;

3. A brief history of the business; and

4. Personal and business financial statements for each partner, officer, director, and stockholder with 20 percent or more ownership.

A contractor's estimate for repairing structural damage may be desirable, but you may make your own cost estimate if you wish.

The U.S. SBA Disaster Business Loan Application is set forth in Appendix 12.

Loans of $10,000 or less do not require collateral. Loans in excess of $10,000 require the pledging of collateral to the extent it is available. Normally the collateral would consist of a first or second mortgage on the damaged business property. The SBA will not decline a loan for lack of collateral, but you must pledge available collateral. The SBA may decline a loan if a business has collateral available but refuses to pledge it.

In addition, the SBA must be satisfied that the business can repay the loan from its operations and will take reasonable safeguards to help ensure that the loan is repaid, e.g., the SBA will require the principals of the business to personally guarantee repayment of the loan.

In order to approve the loan, the SBA must first estimate the cost of repairing the damage. Once you have returned your loan application, an SBA loss verifier will visit you to determine the extent of the damage and the cost to repair or replace it.

The SBA tries to issue a decision on a loan application within 7 to 21 days after receiving the completed application. If the loan is approved, the SBA will tell you what documents are needed to close the loan. Once those documents are provided, the SBA will disburse the funds in installments, as needed to repair or replace the damage.

USE OF FUNDS

The maximum amount your business may borrow for any one disaster is limited to $1.5 million for both physical damage and economic injury combined. The penalty for misusing SBA disaster funds is immediate repayment of one-and-a-half times the original amount of the loan.

Physical Damage

The disaster loan is intended to help you return your business property to its pre-disaster condition. Repair or replacement of real property, machinery, equipment, fixtures, inventory and leasehold improvements may be included in the loan. In addition, disaster loans to repair or replace real property or leasehold improvements may be increased by as much as 20 percent to protect the damaged real property against possible future disasters of the same type.

Normally, SBA funds cannot be used to expand or upgrade a business. If, however, city or county building codes require you to upgrade, then you can use the SBA loan proceeds for that purpose. The SBA requires that you obtain receipts and maintain good records of all loan expenditures as you restore your damaged property, and that you keep these receipts and records for three years. If your business is completely destroyed, limited relocation costs can be included in the loan amount.

Economic Injury

The economic injury portion of the loan will provide you with operating funds until your business recovers. The economic injury loan is intended to help you maintain a secure financial condition until your business is back to normal. To the extent you could have made payments had the disaster not occurred, you may use the loan to make payments on short-term notes, accounts payable and installment payments on long-term notes.

You may not use SBA funds to pay cash dividends or bonuses, or for disbursements to owners, partners, officers or stockholders not directly related to the performance of services for the business. Further, the SBA will not refinance long-term debts or provide working capital that was needed by the business prior to the disaster.

In determining the amount of funds attributable to economic loss, the eligible amount may not be in excess of what your business could have paid had the disaster not occurred. In order for the SBA to compare your financial condition and operating results preceding the disaster with those during and since the disaster period, you must furnish balance sheets and operating statements for similar periods of time.

In addition, the business and its principal owners must use private credit sources, such as bank loans, as well as their own resources to overcome the economic injury to the greatest extent possible without causing undue hardship.

In determining your eligible amount, the SBA will consider the following factors

1. The total of your debt obligations;

2. Operating expenses that mature during the period affected by the disaster;

3. The amount you need to maintain a reasonable working capital position during the period affected by the disaster; and

4. The expenses you could have met and a working capital position you could have maintained had the disaster not occurred.

The amount of your economic injury does not automatically represent the dollar amount of your loan eligibility. The SBA will evaluate the information you provide and determine the reasonableness of your loan request. In addition, the SBA will review the availability of assets to determine if part or all of your economic injury might be remedied by using such assets.

LOAN TERMS

The SBA will assess your financial situation and will set loan terms based on your needs and repayment ability. The maximum maturity for disaster loans is 30 years. However, the actual maturity is based on your ability to repay the loan.

The interest rate that the SBA charges on a disaster loan is determined by your ability to obtain credit elsewhere, i.e., from non-federal sources. If the SBA determines that the business is unable to obtain credit elsewhere, the law sets a maximum interest rate of 4 percent per year.

For businesses that the SBA has determined are able to obtain credit elsewhere, the interest rate cannot exceed that being charged in the private market at the time of the physical disaster or 8 percent, whichever is less. The maturity of this loan cannot exceed three years.

THE MILITARY RESERVIST ECONOMIC INJURY DISASTER LOAN PROGRAM

The purpose of the Military Reservist Economic Injury Disaster Loan program (MREIDL) is to provide funds to eligible small businesses to meet its ordinary and necessary operating expenses that it could have met, but is unable to meet, because an essential employee was "called-up" to active duty in their role as a military reservist. An essential employee is an individual—whether or not an owner of the small business—whose managerial or technical expertise is critical to the successful day-to-day operations of the small business.

The program applies to military conflicts occurring or ending on or after March 24, 1999. The period of military conflict refers to: (1) a period of war declared by Congress; or (2) a period of national emergency declared by the Congress or the President; or (3) a period of contingency operation. A contingency operation is designated by the Secretary of Defense as an operation in which the military may become involved in military action, operations, or hostilities, e.g., peace keeping operations.

Use of Funds

These loans are intended only to provide the amount of working capital needed by a small business to pay its necessary obligations as they mature until operations return to normal after the essential employee is released from active military duty. The purpose of these loans is not to cover lost income or lost profits. MREIDL funds cannot be used to take the place of regular commercial debt, to refinance long-term debt or to expand the business.

Federal law requires the SBA to determine whether credit in an amount needed to accomplish full recovery is available from non-government sources without creating an undue financial hardship to the applicant. Because the Military Reservist economic injury loans are taxpayer subsidized, Congress intended that applicants with the financial capacity to fund their own recovery should do so and therefore are not eligible for MREIDL assistance.

Generally, the SBA determines that over 90% of disaster loan applicants do not have sufficient financial resources to recover without the assistance of the Federal government.

Loans of $5,000 or less do not require collateral. Loans in excess of $5,000 require the pledging of collateral to the extent that it is available. Normally the collateral would consist of a first or second mortgage on the business property. In addition, personal guaranties by the principals of the business are required. The SBA will not decline a loan for lack of collateral, but you must pledge available collateral.

Loan Terms

Interest rates are determined by formulas set by law and recalculated quarterly. The maximum interest rate for this program is 4%. In addition, the law authorizes loan terms up to a maximum of 30 years. Nevertheless, the SBA determines the term of each loan in accordance with the borrower's ability to repay. Based on the financial circumstances of each borrower, the SBA determines an appropriate installment payment amount, which in turn determines the actual term.

The maximum loan amount is $1,500,000. The actual amount of each loan, up to this maximum, is limited to the actual economic injury as calculated by the SBA, not compensated by business interruption insurance or otherwise, and beyond the ability of the business and/or its owners to provide. If a business is a major source of employment, the SBA has authority to waive the $1,500,000 statutory limit.

The Filing Period for small businesses to apply for economic injury loan assistance begins on the date the essential employee is ordered to active duty and ends on the date 90 days after the essential employee is discharged or released from active duty.

Documentation

In addition to the documentation that must accompany the loan application, as set forth above, the military reservist must submit the following:

1. A copy of the essential employee's orders for active duty or copy of their discharge or release papers from active duty status;

2. A statement from the small business owner that the reservist is essential to the day-to-day operations of the business along with a written concurrence by the essential employee;

3. A written explanation and estimate of how the essential employee's activation to military service has or will result in the small business experiencing substantial economic injury;

4. A description of the steps the business is taking to alleviate the substantial economic injury; and

5. A certification from the small business owner that the essential employee will be offered the same job or similar job upon the employee's return from active duty.

THE SBA DISASTER OFFICES

The SBA has disaster offices located strategically around the country, They include: (1) The Disaster Assistance Customer Service Center (CSC) (2) The Field Operations Center – East (FOC-E); (3) The Field Operations Center – West (FOC-W); and (4) The Disaster Assistance Processing and Disbursement Center (PDC);

The SBA Disaster Assistance Customer Service Center

The SBA Disaster Assistance Customer Service Center (CSC) is the contact center supporting the customer service needs of the SBA's Office of Disaster Assistance by providing a single resource for its customers. Contact information is as follows:

The SBA Disaster Assistance Customer Service Center

130 South Elmwood Avenue, Suite 516

Buffalo, New York 14202

Tel: 716-843-4100/Toll-Free: 800-659-2955

Fax: 716-848-4281

Email: disastercustomerservice@sba.gov

The SBA Field Operations Center – East (FOC-E)

The SBA Field Operations Center – East (FOC-E) manages and coordinates field response and all field resources necessary to implement the SBA's Disaster Loan Program within their respective jurisdictions. FOC-E is responsible for conducting original verifications of disaster damages outside the continental United States. They are also responsible for conducting all Preliminary Damage Assessments, re-verifications, and progress inspections in their respective geographical areas of responsibility both inside/outside the continental United States. They also respond to congressional inquiries and perform public information functions.

FOC-E serves the states east of the Mississippi River, plus Minnesota, the U.S. Virgin Islands, and the Commonwealth of Puerto Rico. Contact information is as follows:

The SBA Field Operations Center - East

One Baltimore Place, Suite 300

Atlanta, Georgia 30308

Telephone: 404-347-3771/Toll Free: 800-659 -2955

Fax: 404-347-4183

The SBA Field Operations Center – West (FOC-W)

The SBA Field Operations Center – West (FOC-w) manages and coordinates field response and all field resources necessary to implement SBA's Disaster Loan Program within their respective jurisdictions. FOC-W is responsible for conducting original verifications of disaster damages outside the continental United States. They are also responsible for conducting all Preliminary Damage Assessments, re-verifications, and progress inspections in their respective geographical areas of responsibility both inside/outside the continental United States. They also respond to congressional inquiries and perform public information functions.

FOC-W serves Alaska, American Samoa, Arizona, California, Colorado, Commonwealth of the Northern Mariana Islands, Federated States of Micronesia, Guam, Hawaii, Idaho, Iowa, Kansas, Louisiana, Missouri, Montana, Nebraska, Nevada, New Mexico, North Dakota, Oklahoma, Oregon, Republic of the Marshall Islands, South Dakota, Texas, Utah, Washington and Wyoming. Contact information is as follows:

The SBA Field Operations Center - West

P.O. Box 419004

Sacramento, CA 95841-9004

916-735-1500/Toll Free: 800-488-5323

The SBA Disaster Assistance Processing and Disbursement Center

The SBA Disaster Assistance Processing and Disbursement Center (PDC) serves all U.S. states, territories, possessions, and commonwealths. All loan applications for SBA Disaster Loan Programs are sent to this office for processing. Application processing functions, from application entry, scanning, and processing through to a decision occur in the PDC. All loan approvals, loan document generation, loan closing, and disbursement of loan proceeds are functions of the PDC. The PDC deploys field loan closers as needed to support loan closing operations. Contact information is as follows:

The SBA Disaster Assistance Processing & Disbursement Center

14925 Kingsport Road

Fort Worth, Texas 76155

Telephone: 817-868-2300/Toll Free: 800-366-6303

Fax: 817-684-5616

APPENDIX 1:
DIRECTORY OF FEDERAL EMERGENCY MANAGEMENT AGENCY – REGIONAL OFFICES

REGION	COVERAGE AREA	ADDRESS	TELEPHONE NUMBER
Region I	CT, ME, MA, NH, RI, VT	99 High Street, 6th Floor, Boston, MA 02110	617-956-7506
Region II	NJ, NY, PR, VI	26 Federal Plaza, Suite 1337, New York, NY 10278-0002	212-680-3600
Region III	DE, DC, MD, PA, VA, WV	615 Chestnut Street, One Independence Mall, Sixth Floor, Philadelphia, PA 19106-4404	215-931-5608
Region IV	AL, FL, GA, KY, MS, NC, SC, TN	3003 Chamblee Tucker Road, Atlanta, GA 30341	770-220-5200
Region V	IL, IN, MI, MN, OH, WI	536 South Clark St., 6th Floor, Chicago, IL 60605	312-408-5500
Region VI	AR, LA, NM, OK, TX	FRC 800 North Loop 288, Dento, TX 76209-3698	940-898-5399
Region VII	IA, KS, MO, NB	9221 Ward Parkway, Suite 300, Kansas City, MO 64114-3372	816-283-7063

REGION	COVERAGE AREA	ADDRESS	TELEPHONE NUMBER
Region VIII	CO, MT, ND, SD, UT, WY	Denver Federal Center, Building 710, box 25267, Denver, CO 80255	303-235-4900
Region IX	AZ, CA, HI, NV, American Samoa, Guam, N. Mariana Islands, Marshall Islands, Micronesia	1111 Broadway, Suite 1200, Oakland, CA 94607-4052	510-627-7100
Region X	AK, ID, OR, WA	Federal Regional Center, 130 228th Street SW, Bothell, WA 98021-8627	425-487-4600

SOURCE: Federal Emergency Management Agency (FEMA)

APPENDIX 2:
DIRECTORY OF STATE OFFICES OF EMERGENCY MANAGEMENT

STATE	ADDRESS	TELEPHONE NUMBER	FAX	WEBSITE
ALABAMA,	Alabama Emergency Management Agency,, 5898 County Road 41,, P.O. Drawer 2160,, Clanton,, Alabama 35046-2160,	(205) 280-2200,	(205) 280-2495,	ema.alabama.gov/
ALASKA,	Alaska Division of Emergency Services,, P.O. Box 5750,, Fort Richardson,, Alaska 99505-5750,	(907) 428-7000,	(907) 428-7009,	www.ak-prepared.com
ARIZONA,	Arizona Division of Emergency Management,, 5636 E. McDowell Rd.,, Phoenix,, Arizona 85008,	(602) 244-0504,	n/a	www.azdema.gov
ARKANSAS,	Arkansas Department of Emergency Management,, P.O. Box 758,, Conway,, Arkansas 72053,	(501) 730-9750,	(501) 730-9754,	www.adem.state.ar.us/
CALIFORNIA,	California Governor's Office of Emergency Services,, 3650 Schriever Ave.,, Mather,, CA 95655-4203,	(916) 845-8510,	(916) 845-8511,	www.oes.ca.gov/

STATE	ADDRESS	TELEPHONE	FAX	WEBSITE
COLORADO,	Colorado Office of Emergency Management,, 9195 East Mineral Avenue,, Suite 200,, Centennial,, Colorado 80112,	(720) 852-6600,	(720) 852-6750,	www.dola.state.co.us/ oem/oemindex.htm
CONNECTICUT,	Connecticut Office of Emergency Management,, 360 Broad Street,, Hartford,, Connecticut 06105,	(860) 566-3180,	(860) 247-0664,	www.ct.gov/demhs/site/ default.asp
DELAWARE,	Delaware Emergency Management Agency,, 165 Brick Store,, Landing Road,, Smyrna,, Delaware 19977,	(302) 659-3362,	(302) 659-6855,	www.state.de.us/dema/ index.htm
DISTRICT OF COLUMBIA,	District of Columbia Emergency Management Agency,, 2000 14th Street NW,, 8th Floor,, Washington,, D.C. 20009,	(202) 727-6161,	(202) 673-2290,	www.dcema.dc.gov
FLORIDA,	Florida Division of Emergency Management,, 2555 Shumard Oak Blvd.,, Tallahassee,, Florida 32399-2100,	(850) 413-9969,	(850) 488-1016,	www.floridadisaster.org
GEORGIA,	Georgia Emergency Management Agency,, P.O. Box 18055,, Atlanta,, Georgia 30316-0055,	(404) 635-7000,	(404) 635-7205,	www. State.Ga.US/GEMA/
HAWAII,	Hawaii State Civil Defense,, 3949 Diamond Head Road,, Honolulu,, Hawaii 96816-4495,	(808) 733-4300,	(808) 733-4287,	www.scd.hawaii.gov
IDAHO,	Idaho Bureau of Disaster Services,, 4040 Guard Street,, Bldg. 600,, Boise, Idaho 83705-5004,	(208) 334-3460,	(208) 334-2322,	www2.state.id.us/bds/

State	Address	Phone	Phone	Website
ILLINOIS,	Illinois Emergency Management Agency,, 2200 S. Dirksen Pkwy.,, Springfield,, Illinois 62703,	(217) 782-2700,	(217) 524-7967,	www.state.il.us/iema
INDIANA,	Indiana Department of Homeland Security,, 302 West Washington Street,, Room E208,, Indianapolis,, Indiana 46204-2767,	(317) 232-3986,	(317) 232-3895,	www.ai.org/sema/index.html
IOWA,	Iowa Homeland Security & Emergency Management Division,, Hoover Office Building,, Des Moines,, Iowa 50319,	(515) 281-3231,	(515) 281-7539,	www.Iowahomelandsecurity.org.
KANSAS,	Kansas Division of Emergency Management,, 2800 S.W. Topeka Boulevard,, Topeka,, Kansas 66611-1287,	(785) 274-1401,	(785) 274-1426,	www.ink.org/public/kdem/
KENTUCKY,	Kentucky Emergency Management,,100 Minuteman Parkway,, Bldg. 100,, Frankfort,, Kentucky 40601-6168,	(502) 607-1682,	(502) 607-1614,	kyem.ky.gov/
LOUISIANA,	Louisiana Office of Emergency Preparedness,, 7667 Independence Blvd.,, Baton Rouge,, Louisiana 70806,	(225) 925-7500,	(225) 925-7501,	www.ohsep.louisiana.gov
MAINE,	Maine Emergency Management Agency,, 45 Commerce Drive,, Suite #2,, #72 State House Station,, Augusta,, Maine 04333-0072,,	207-624-4400,,	207-287-3180,	www.state.me.us/mema/memahome.htm
MICHIGAN,	Michigan Dept. of State Police, 4000 Collins Road,, Lansing,, MI 48910,, (517) 333-5042,	(517) 333-4987,		www.michigan.gov/emd
MARYLAND,	Maryland Emergency Management Agency,, 5401 Rue Saint Lo Drive,, Reistertown,, Maryland 21136,	(410) 517-3600,	(410) 517-3610,	www.mema.state.md.us/

STATE	ADDRESS	TELEPHONE	FAX	WEBSITE
MASSACHUSETTS,	Massachusetts Emergency Management Agency,, 400 Worcester Road,, Framingham,, Massachusetts 01702-5399,	(508) 820-2000,	(508) 820-2030,	www.state.ma.us/mema
MICHIGAN,	Michigan Division of Emergency Management,, 4000 Collins Road,, P.O. Box 30636,, Lansing, Michigan 48909-8136,	(517) 333-5042,	(517) 333-4987,	www.michigan.gov/msp/1,1607,7-123-1593_3507—,00.html
MINNESOTA,	Minnesota Homeland Security and Emergency Management Division,, 444 Cedar Street,, Suite 223,, St. Paul,, MN 55101-6223,	(651) 296-0466,	(651) 296-0459,	www.hsem.state.mn.us
MISSISSIPPI,	Mississippi Emergency Management Agency,, P.O. Box 4501 - Fondren Station,, Jackson,, Mississippi 39296-4501,	(601) 352-9100,	(601) 352-8314,	www.www.msema.org
MISSOURI,	Missouri Emergency Management Agency,, P.O. Box 116,, 2302 Militia Drive,, Jefferson City,, Missouri 65102,,	(573) 526-9100,	(573) 634-7966,	www.sema.dps.mo.gov
MONTANA,	Montana Division of Disaster & Emergency Services,, 1900 Williams Street,, Helena,, Montana 59604-4789,	(406) 841-3911,	(406) 444-3965,	www.dma.mt.gov/des/
NEBRASKA,	Nebraska Emergency Management Agency,, 1300 Military Road,, Lincoln,, Nebraska 68508-1090,	(402) 471-7410,	(402) 471-7433,	www.nema.ne.gov
NEVADA,	Nevada Division of Emergency Management,, 2525 South Carson Street, Carson City,, Nevada 89711,	(775) 687-4240,	(775) 687-6788,	www.dem.state.nv.us/

NEW HAMPSHIRE,	Governor's Office of Emergency Management,, 107 Pleasant Street, Concord,, New Hampshire 03301,	(603) 271-2231,	(603) 225-7341,	www.nhoem.state.nh.us/
NEW JERSEY,	New Jersey Office of Emergency Management,, P.O. Box 7068,, West Trenton,, New Jersey 08628-0068,	(609) 538-6050,	(609) 538-0345,	www. state.nj.us/oem/county/
NEW MEXICO,	New Mexico Office of Emergency Management,, P.O. Box 1628,, 13 Bataan Boulevard,, Santa Fe,, New Mexico 87505,	(505) 476-9600,	(505) 476-9695,	www.dps.nm.org/ emergency/index.htm
NEW YORK,	New York State Emergency Management Office,, 1220 Washington Avenue,, Building 22,, Suite 101,, Albany,, New York 12226-2251,	(518) 292-2275,	v(518) 457-9995,	www.nysemo.state. ny.us/
NORTH CAROLINA,	North Carolina Division of Emergency Management,, 4713 Mail Service Center,, Raleigh,, NC 27699-4713,	(919) 733-3867,	(919) 733-5406,	www.dem.dcc.state.nc. us/
NORTH DAKOTA,	North Dakota Department of Emergency Services,, P.O. Box 5511,, Bismarck,, North Dakota 58506-5511,	(701) 328-8100,	701) 328-8181,	(www.nd.gov/des
OHIO,	Ohio Emergency Management Agency,, 2855 West Dublin-Granville Road,, Columbus,, Ohio 43235-2206,	(614) 889-7150,	(614) 889-7183,	www.ema.ohio.gov/ema. asp
OKLAHOMA,	Office of Civil Emergency Management, Will Rogers Sequoia Tunnel,, 2401 N. Lincoln,, Oklahoma City,, Oklahoma 73152,	(405) 521-2481,	(405) 521-4053,	www.odcem.state.ok.us/

STATE	ADDRESS	TELEPHONE	FAX	WEBSITE
OREGON,	Oregon Emergency Management,, P.O. Box 14370,, Salem,, Oregon 97309-5062,	(503) 378-2911,	(503) 373-7833,	egov. oregon.gov/OOHS/OEM
PENNSYLVANIA,	Pennsylvania Emergency Management Agency,, 2605 Interstate Drive,, Harrisburg,, PA 17110-9463,	(717) 651-2001,	(717) 651-2040,	www.pema.state.pa.us/
RHODE ISLAND,	Rhode Island Emergency Management Agency,, 645 New London Ave.,, Cranston,, Rhode Island 02920-3003,	(401) 946-9996,	(401) 944-1891,	www.riema.ri.gov
SOUTH CAROLINA,	South Carolina Emergency Management Division,, 2779 Fish Hatchery Road,, West Columbia,, South Carolina 29172,,	(803) 737-8500,	(803) 737-8570,	www.scemd.org/
SOUTH DAKOTA,	South Dakota Division of Emergency Management,, 118 West Capitol,, Pierre,, South Dakota 57501,	(605) 773-3231,	(605) 773-3580,	www.state.sd.us/dps/ sddem/home.htm
TENNESSEE,	Tennessee Emergency Management Agency,, 3041 Sidco Drive,, Nashville,, Tennessee 37204-1502,	(615) 741-4332,	(615) 242-9635,	www.tnema.org
TEXAS,	Texas Division of Emergency Management,, 5805 N. Lamar,, Austin,, Texas 78752,	(512) 424-2138,	(512) 424-7160,	www. txdps.state.tx.us/dem/

State	Address			Website
UTAH,	Utah Division of Emergency Services and Homeland Security,, 1110 State Office Building,, P.O. Box 141710, Salt Lake City,, Utah 84114-1710,	(801) 538-3400,	(801) 538-3770,	www.des.utah.gov
VERMONT,	Vermont Emergency Management Agency,, 103 South Main Street,, Waterbury,, Vermont 05671-2101,	(802) 244-8721,	(802) 244-8655,	www.dps.state.vt.us/
VIRGINIA,	Virginia Department of Emergency Management,, 10501 Trade Court Richmond,, VA 23236-3713,	(804) 897-6502,	(804) 897-6506,	www.vdem.state.va.us
WASHINGTON,	State of Washington Emergency Management Division,, Building 20,, M/S: TA-20,, Camp Murray,, Washington 98430-5122,	(253) 512-7000,	(253) 512-7200,	www.emd.wa.gov/
WEST VIRGINIA,	West Virginia Office of Emergency Services,, Building 1,, Room EB-80,, 1900 Kanawha Boulevard,, East Charleston,, West Virginia 25305-0360,	(304) 558-5380,	(304) 344-4538,	www.wvdhsem.gov
WISCONSIN,	Wisconsin Emergency Management,, 2400 Wright Street,, P.O. Box 7865,, Madison.. Wisconsin 53707-7865,	(608) 242-3232,	(608) 242-3247	emergencymanagement. wi.gov/
WYOMING,	Wyoming Office of Homeland Security,, 122 W. 25th Street,, Cheyenne, Wyoming 82002,	(307) 777-4900,	(307) 635-6017	wyohomelandsecurity. state.wy.us

SOURCE: Federal Emergency Management Agency (FEMA)

APPENDIX 3:
BUSINESS CONTINUITY ACRONYMS

ABCI	Associate of the Business Continuity Institute
ABCP	Associate Business Continuity Professional
ACD	Automatic Call Distribution
ACP	Association of Contingency Planners, Access Control Point
ALE	Annual Loss Expectancy
ANSI	American National Standards Institute
ARC	American Red Cross
BCC	Business Continuity Coordinator
BCI	Business Continuity Institute
BCM	Business Continuity Management
BCP	Business Continuity Plan
BIA	Business Impact Analysis
BIRRA	Business Impact Resource Recovery Analysis (BCI)
BRC	British Red Cross
BRC	Business Recovery Coordinator
BRF	Business Recovery Facility
BRP	Business Resumption Planning
BS	British Standard
CAT	Crisis Action Team
CBCP	Certified Business Continuity Professional
CBRM	Certified Business Resilience Manager
CD	Civil Defense

CDC	Centers for Disease Control (US)
CDRG	Catastrophic Disaster Response Group (FEMA)
CDRP	Certified Disaster Recovery Planner
CEAS	Corporate Emergency Access System (NY)
CEM	Certified Emergency Manager
CEMP	Comprehensive Emergency Management Program
CERT	Community Emergency Response Team
CFCP	Certified Functional Continuity Professional
CM	Crisis Management
CMT	Crisis Management Team
COBIT	Control Objectives for Information and Related Technologies
COOP	Continuity of Operations Plan
COSO	Committee of Sponsoring Organizations
CP	Contingency Plan, Contingency Planning
CPG	Civil Preparedness Guide
CPU	Central Processing Unit
CRP	Certified Recovery Planner
CRSA	Control & Risk Self Assessment (BCI)
DASD	Direct Access Storage Device
DBMS	Database Management System
DFO	Disaster Field Office (FEMA)
DHS	Department of Homeland Security (US)
DID	Direct Inward Dial
DOD	Department of Defense (US)
DOH	Department of Health (US)
DOT	Department of Transportation (US)
DR	Disaster Recovery
DRC	Disaster Recovery Coordinator
DRJ	Disaster Recovery Journal
DRII	Disaster Recovery Institute International
DRP	Disaster Recovery Plan, Disaster Recovery Planning
DNS	Domain Naming Server, Domain Naming System
EAB	Editorial Advisory Board
EBS	Emergency Broadcast System

ECC	Emergency Control Center (BCI)
EM	Emergency Management
EMA	Emergency Management Agency
EMT	Emergency Management Team
EO	Executive Oder (US)
EOC	Emergency Operations Center
EPA	Environmental Protection Agency (US)
EPO	Emergency Planning Officer (BCI)
ER	Emergency Response
ERC	Employee Relief Center
ERT	Emergency Response Team (FEMA)
ERT-A	Emergency Response Team—Advance Element (FEMA)
ESF	Emergency Support Function (FEMA)
ESS	Enterprise Storage System
EST	Emergency Support Team (FEMA)
ETR	Estimated Time to Recovery
EZ	Exclusion Zone (BCI)
FAA	Federal Aviation Administration (US)
FAX	Facsimile
FBCI	Fellow of the Business Continuity Institute
FCC	Federal Communications Commission (US)
FCO	Federal Coordinating Officer (FEMA)
FCPA	Foreign Corrupt Practices Act (US)
FDA	Food and Drug Administration (US)
FEMA	Federal Emergency Management Agency (US)
FFIEC	Federal Financial Institutions Examination Council
FIRM	Flood Insurance Rate Maps
FNMA	Federal National Mortgage Association
FSA	Financial Services Authority (BCI)
GAP	Generally Accepted Practices
GE	General Emergency
GIS	Geographic Information System
GNMA	Government National Mortgage Association
GSA	General Services Administration (US)
HA	High Availability

HAZMAT	Hazardous Materials
HHS	Department of Health & Human Services (US)
HIPAA	Health Insurance Portability and Accountability Act (1996)
HMTUSA	Hazardous Materials Transportation Uniform Safety Act
HRDR	Human Resources Disaster Recovery
HSPD	Homeland Security Presidential Directive
HVAC	Heating, Ventilating, and Air Conditioning
ICRC	International Committee of the Red Cross
ICS	Incident Command System
IM	Information Management
IMP	Incident Management Plan
IMT	Information Management Team
I/O	Input/Output
IP	Internet Protocol
IPT	Internet Protocol Telephony
ISO	International Standards Organization
IT	Information Technology
ITIL	Information Technology Information Library
JIC	Joint Information Center
KI	Potassium Iodide (Thyroid Blocking Agent)
LAN	Local Area Network
LEC	Local Exchange Carrier
MBCI	Member of the Business Continuity Institute
MBCP	Master Business Continuity Professional
MICR	Magnetic Ink Character Recognition
MODEM	Modulator Demodulator
MSDS	Material Safety Data Sheet
MTO	Maximum Tolerable Outage (BCI)
MTPD	Maximum Tolerable Period of Disruption (BCI)
NANPA	North American Numbering Plan Administration
NAWAS	National Warning System
NECC	National Emergency Coordination Center (FEMA)
NFIP	National Flood Insurance Program
NFPA	National Fire Protectional Agency (US)

NIMS	National Incident Management System (US)
NLEEC	National Law Enforcement Emergency Channel
NOAA	National Oceanic and Atmospheric Association
NRP	National Recovery Plan
NTSB	National Transportation Safety Board (US)
NWS	National Weather Service
OLTP	Online Transaction Processing
OPS	Operations
OLA	Operational Level Agreement
OSHA	Occupational Safety & Health Administration (US)
PBX	Private Branch Exchange
PDD	Presidential Decision Directive
PEST	Political/Environment/Social/Technical Analysis (BCI)
PIO	Public Information Officer
PMP	Project Manager Professional
PPBI	Public & Private Businesses, Inc
PP	Professional Practices
PMI	Project Management Institute
PTSD	Post Traumatic Stress Disorder
PTT	Push To Talk
RAID	Redundant Array of Inexpensive Disk
ROC	Regional Operations Center (FEMA)
RPO	Recovery Point Objective
RTO	Recovery Time Objective
RA	Risk Assessment
RVP	Rendezvous Point (BCI)
SAN	Storage Area Network
SBA	Small Business Association
SBCI	Specialist of the Business Continuity Institute
SCO	State Coordinating Officer (FEMA)
SEMO	State Emergency Management Office
SFHAs	Special Flood Hazard Areas
SITREPs	Situation Reports
SLA	Service Level Agreement
SLM	Service Level Management

SOP	Standard Operating Procedure
SOX	Sarbanes-Oxley
SQL	Structured Query Language
SWOT	Strengths/Weaknesses/Opportunities/Threat Analysis (BCI)
2PC	Two Phase Commit
TIA	Technical Impact Analysis
TNA	Training Needs Analysis
TVSS	Transient Voltage Surge Suppression
UBC	Uniform Building Code
UPS	Uninterruptible Power Supply
URL	Universal Resource Locator
USACE	US Army Corps of Engineers (US)
USCG	United States Coast Guard
USDA	United States Department of Agriculture (US)
USGS	United States Geological Survey
VA	Veteran's Administration (US)
VPN	Virtual Private Network
VSAT	Very Small Aperture Terminal
WAN	Wide Area Network
WHO	World Health Organization
WMD	Weapons of Mass Destruction
WRC	Work Recovery Center

SOURCE: Disaster Recovery Journal and DRI: The Institute for Continuity Management

APPENDIX 4:
SAMPLE EMERGENCY PLAN

Ready Business
Prepare. Plan. Stay Informed.

Sample Emergency Plan

Sample Business Continuity and Disaster Preparedness Plan

☐ **PLAN TO STAY IN BUSINESS**

If this location is not accessible we will operate from location below:

Business Name   Business Name

Address   Address

City, State   City, State

Telephone Number   Telephone Number

The following person is our primary crisis manager and will serve as the company spokesperson in an emergency.

If the person is unable to manage the crisis, the person below will succeed in management:

Primary Emergency Contact   Secondary Emergency Contact

Telephone Number   Telephone Number

Alternative Number   Alternative Number

E-mail   E-mail

☐ **EMERGENCY CONTACT INFORMATION**

Dial 9-1-1 in an Emergency

Non-Emergency Police/Fire

Insurance Provider

Sample Emergency Plan

Sample Business Continuity and Disaster Preparedness Plan (cont'd)

☐ **BE INFORMED**

The following natural and man-made disasters could impact our business.

o _____
o _____
o _____
o _____

☐ **EMERGENCY PLANNING TEAM**

The following people will participate in emergency planning and crisis management.

o _____
o _____
o _____
o _____
o _____

☐ **WE PLAN TO COORDINATE WITH OTHERS**

The following people from neighboring businesses and our building management will participate on our emergency planning team.

o _____
o _____
o _____
o _____
o _____

☐ **OUR CRITICAL OPERATIONS**

The following is a prioritized list of our critical operations, staff and procedures we need to recover from a disaster.

Operation	Staff in Charge	Action Plan
_____	_____	_____
_____	_____	_____
_____	_____	_____
_____	_____	_____

Sample Emergency Plan

Sample Business Continuity and Disaster Preparedness Plan (cont'd)

☐ SUPPLIERS AND CONTRACTORS

Company Name: _____

Street Address: _____

City: _____ State: _____ Zip Code: _____

Phone: _____ Fax: _____ E-Mail: _____

Contact Name: _____ Account Number: _____

Materials/Service Provided: _____

If this company experiences a disaster, we will obtain supplies/materials from the following:

Company Name: _____

Street Address: _____

City: _____ State: _____ Zip Code: _____

Phone: _____ Fax: _____ E-Mail: _____

Contact Name: _____ Account Number: _____

Materials/Service Provided: _____

If this company experiences a disaster, we will obtain supplies/materials from the following:

Company Name: _____

Street Address: _____

City: _____ State: _____ Zip Code: _____

Phone: _____ Fax: _____ E-Mail: _____

Contact Name: _____ Account Number: _____

Materials/Service Provided: _____

Sample Emergency Plan

Sample Business Continuity and Disaster Preparedness Plan (cont'd)

☐ **EVACUATION PLAN FOR** _____ **LOCATION**

(Insert address)

- o We have developed these plans in collaboration with neighboring businesses and building owners to avoid confusion or gridlock.
- o We have located, copied and posted building and site maps.
- o Exits are clearly marked.
- o We will practice evacuation procedures _____ times a year.

If we must leave the workplace quickly:

_____
_____

1. Warning System:_____

   We will test the warning system and record results _____ times a year.

2. Assembly Site: _____

3. Assembly Site Manager & Alternate:_____

   a. Responsibilities Include:

   _____
   _____
   _____

4. Shut Down Manager & Alternate:_____

   a. Responsibilities Include:

   _____
   _____
   _____

5. _____ is responsible for issuing all clear.

Sample Emergency Plan

Sample Business Continuity and Disaster Preparedness Plan (cont'd)

☐ **SHELTER-IN-PLACE PLAN FOR** _____ **LOCATION**
                                    (Insert address)

    o We have talked to co-workers about which emergency supplies, if any, the company will provide in the shelter location and which supplies individuals might consider keeping in a portable kit personalized for individual needs.

    o We will practice shelter procedures ____ times a year.

If we must take shelter quickly

_____

_____

1. Warning System:_____

   We will test the warning system and record results ____ times a year.

2. Storm Shelter Location: _____

3. "Seal the Room" Shelter Location:_____

4. Shelter Manager & Alternate:

    a. Responsibilities Include:

    _____

    _____

    _____

5. Shut Down Manager & Alternate:

    a. Responsibilities Include:

    _____

    _____

    _____

6. _____is responsible for issuing all clear.

Sample Emergency Plan

Sample Business Continuity and Disaster Preparedness Plan (cont'd)

☐ COMMUNICATIONS

We will communicate our emergency plans with co-workers in the following way:

_____
_____

In the event of a disaster we will communicate with employees in the following way:

_____
_____

☐ CYBER SECURITY

To protect our computer hardware, we will:

_____

To protect our computer software, we will:

_____

If our computers are destroyed, we will use back-up computers at the following location:

_____

☐ RECORDS BACK-UP

_____ is responsible for backing up our critical records including payroll and accounting systems.

Back-up records including a copy of this plan, site maps, insurance policies, bank account records and computer back ups are stored onsite _____.

Another set of back-up records is stored at the following off-site location:

_____

If our accounting and payroll records are destroyed, we will provide for continuity in the following ways:

_____

Sample Business Continuity and Disaster Preparedness Plan (cont'd)

☐ **EMPLOYEE EMERGENCY CONTACT INFORMATION**

The following is a list of our co-workers and their individual emergency contact information:

_____	_____	_____
_____	_____	_____
_____	_____	_____
_____	_____	_____

☐ **ANNUAL REVIEW**

We will review and update this business continuity and disaster plan in _____.

APPENDIX 5:
EMERGENCY SUPPLIES CHECKLIST

 **Ready** Business
Prepare. Plan. Stay Informed.

Emergency Supplies

Emergency Supplies

Talk to your co-workers about what emergency supplies the company can feasibly provide, if any, and which ones individuals should consider keeping on hand. Recommended emergency supplies include the following:

	Water, amounts for portable kits will vary. Individuals should determine what amount they are able to both store comfortably and to transport to other locations. If it is feasible, store one gallon of water per person per day, for drinking and sanitation
	Food, at least a three-day supply of non-perishable food
	Battery-powered radio and **extra batteries**
	Flashlight and **extra batteries**
	First Aid kit
	Whistle to signal for help
	Dust or filter masks, readily available in hardware stores, which are rated based on how small a particle they filter
	Moist towelettes for sanitation
	Wrench or **pliers** to turn off utilities
	Can opener for food (if kit contains canned food)
	Plastic sheeting and **duct tape** to "seal the room"
	Garbage bags and **plastic ties** for personal sanitation

APPENDIX 6:
COMPUTER INVENTORY FORM

Ready Business
Prepare. Plan. Stay Informed.

Computer Inventory Form

Open for Business Worksheet
Computer Hardware Inventory

Use this form to:

* Log your computer hardware serial and model numbers. Attach a copy of your vendor documentation to this document.
* Record the name of the company from which you purchased or leased this equipment and the contact name to notify for your computer repairs.
* Record the name of the company that provides repair and support for your computer hardware.

Make additional copies as needed.
Keep one copy of this list in a secure place on your premises and another in an off-site location.

HARDWARE INVENTORY LIST

Hardware (CPU, Monitor, Printer, Keyboard, Mouse)	Hardware Size, RAM & CPU Capacity	Model Purchased	Serial Number	Date Purchased	Cost

APPENDIX 7:
LIST OF HAZARDOUS CHEMICALS

Acetaldehyde
Acrolein (2-Popenal)
Acrylyl Chlorde
Allyl Chlorid
Allylamine
Alkylaluminum
Ammonia, Anhydrous
Ammonia solutions (greater than 44% ammonia by weight)
Ammonium Perchlorate
Ammonium Permanganate
Arsine (also called Arsenic Hydride)
Bis (Chloromethyl) Ether
Boron Trichloride
Boron Trifluoride
Bromine
Bromine Chloride
Bromine Pentafluoride
Bromine Trifluoride
3-Bromopropyne (also called Propargyl Bromide)
Butyl Hydroperoxide (Tertiary)

Butyl Perbenzoate (Tertiary)
Carbonyl Chloride
Carbonyl Fluoride
Cellulose Nitrate (concentration greater than 12.6% nitrogen)
Chlorine
Chlorine Dioxide
Chlorine Pentrafluoride
Chlorine Trifluoride
Chlorodiethylaluminum (also called Diethylaluminum Chloride)
1-Chloro-2,4-Dinitrobenzene
Chloromethyl Methyl Ether
Chloropicrin
Chloropicrin and Methyl Bromide mixture
Chloropicrin and Methyl Chloride mixture
Cumene Hydroperoxide
Cyanogen
Cyanogen Chloride
Cyanuric Fluoride
Diacetyl Peroxide (concentration greater than 70%)
Diazomethane
Dibenzoyl Peroxide
Diborane
Dibutyl Peroxide (Tertiary)
Dichloro Acetylene
Dichlorosilane
Diethylzinc
Diisopropyl Peroxydicarbonate
Dilauroyl Peroxide
Dimethyldichlorosilane

Dimethylhydrazine
Dimethylamine, Anhydrous
2,4-Dinitroaniline
Ethyl Methyl Ketone Peroxide
Ethyl Nitrite
Ethylamine
Ethylene Fluorohydrin
Ethylene Oxide
Ethyleneimine
Fluorine
Formaldehyde (Formalin)
Furan
Hexafluoroacetone
Hydrochloric Acid, Anhydrous
Hydrofluoric Acid, Anhydrous
Hydrogen Bromide
Hydrogen Chloride
Hydrogen Cyanide, Anhydrous
Hydrogen Fluoride
Hydrogen Peroxide (52% by weight or greater)
Hydrogen Selenide
Hydrogen Sulfide
Hydroxylamine
Iron, Pentacarbonyl
Isopropylamine
Ketene
Methacrylaldehyde
Methacryloyl Chloride
Methacryloyloxyethyl Isocyanate

Methyl Acrylonitrile
Methylamine, Anhydrous
Methyl Bromide
Methyl Chloride
Methyl Chloroformate
Methyl Ethyl Ketone Peroxide (concentration greater than 60%)
Methyl Fluoroacetate
Methyl Fluorosulfate
Methyl Hydrazine
Methyl Iodide
Methyl Isocyanate
Methyl Mercaptan
Methyl Vinyl Ketone
Methyltrichlorosilane
Nickel Carbonly (Nickel Tetracarbonyl)
Nitric Acid (94.5% by weight or greater)
Nitric Oxide
Nitroaniline
Nitromethane
Nitrogen Dioxide
Nitrogen Oxides (NO; NO(2); N2O4; N2O3)
Nitrogen Tetroxide (also called Nitrogen Peroxide)
Nitrogen Trifluoride
Nitrogen Trioxide
Oleum (65% to 80% by weight; also called Fuming Sulfuric Acid)
Osmium Tetroxide
Oxygen Difluoride (Fluorine Monoxide)
Ozone
Pentaborane

Peracetic Acid (concentration greater 60% Acetic Acid; also called Peroxyacetic Acid)
Perchloric Acid (concentration greater than 60% by weight)
Perchloromethyl Mercaptan
Perchloryl Fluoride
Peroxyacetic Acid (concentration greater than 60% Acetic Acid; also called Peracetic Acid)
Phosgene (also called Carbonyl Chloride)
Phosphine (Hydrogen Phosphide)
Phosphorus Oxychloride (also called Phosphoryl Chloride)
Phosphorus Trichloride
Phosphoryl Chloride (also called Phosphorus Oxychloride)
Propargyl Bromide
Propyl Nitrate
Sarin
Selenium Hexafluoride
Stibine (Antimony Hydride)
Sulfur Dioxide (liquid)
Sulfur Pentafluoride
Sulfur Tetrafluoride
Sulfur Trioxide (also called Sulfuric Anhydride)
Sulfuric Anhydride (also called Sulfur Trioxide)
Tellurium Hexafluoride
Tetrafluoroethylene
Tetrafluorohydrazine
Tetramethyl Lead
Thionyl Chloride
Trichloro (chloromethyl)
Silane
Trichloro (dichlorophenyl)

Silane
Trichlorosilane
Trifluorochloroethylene
Trimethyoxysilane

SOURCE: Occupational Safety and Health Administration (OSHA)

APPENDIX 8:
CHECKLIST FOR PANDEMIC PLANNING

SECTION 1: PLAN FOR THE IMPACT OF A PANDEMIC ON YOUR BUSINESS

1. Identify a pandemic coordinator and/or team with defined roles and responsibilities for preparedness and response planning. The planning process should include input from labor representatives.

2. Identify essential employees and other critical inputs (e.g. raw materials, suppliers, sub-contractor services/ products, and logistics) required to maintain business operations by location and function during a pandemic.

3. Train and prepare ancillary workforce (e.g. contractors, employees in other job titles/descriptions, retirees).

4. Develop and plan for scenarios likely to result in an increase or decrease in demand for your products and/or services during a pandemic (e.g. effect of restriction on mass gatherings, need for hygiene supplies).

5. Determine potential impact of a pandemic on company business financials using multiple possible scenarios that affect different product lines and/or production sites.

6. Determine potential impact of a pandemic on business-related domestic and international travel (e.g. quarantines, border closures).

7. Find up-to-date, reliable pandemic information from community public health, emergency management, and other sources and make sustainable links.

8. Establish an emergency communications plan and revise periodically. This plan includes identification of key contacts (with back-ups), chain of communications (including suppliers and customers), and processes for tracking and communicating business and employee status.

9. Implement an exercise/drill to test your plan, and revise periodically.

SECTION 2: PLAN FOR THE IMPACT OF A PANDEMIC ON YOUR EMPLOYEES AND CUSTOMERS

1. Forecast and allow for employee absences during a pandemic due to factors such as personal illness, family member illness, community containment measures and quarantines, school and/or business closures, and public transportation closures.

2. Implement guidelines to modify the frequency and type of face-to-face contact (e.g. hand-shaking, seating in meetings, office layout, shared workstations) among employees and between employees and customers (refer to CDC recommendations).

3. Encourage and track annual influenza vaccinations for employees.

4. Evaluate employee access to and availability of healthcare services during a pandemic, and improve services as needed.

5. Evaluate employee access to and availability of mental health and social services during a pandemic, including corporate, community, and faith-based resources, and improve services as needed.

6. Identify employees and key customers with special needs, and incorporate the requirements of such persons into your preparedness plan.

SECTION 3: ESTABLISH POLICIES TO BE IMPLEMENTED DURING A PANDEMIC

1. Establish policies for employee compensation and sick-leave absences unique to a pandemic (e.g. non-punitive, liberal leave), including policies on when a previously ill person is no longer infectious and can return to work after illness.

2. Establish policies for flexible worksite (e.g. telecommuting) and flexible work hours (e.g. staggered shifts).

3. Establish policies for preventing influenza spread at the worksite (e.g. promoting respiratory hygiene/ cough etiquette, and prompt exclusion of people with influenza symptoms).

4. Establish policies for employees who have been exposed to pandemic influenza, are suspected to be ill, or become ill at the worksite (e.g. infection control response, immediate mandatory sick leave).

5. Establish policies for restricting travel to affected geographic areas (consider both domestic and international sites), evacuating

employees working in or near an affected area when an outbreak begins, and guidance for employees returning from affected areas (refer to CDC travel recommendations).

6. Set up authorities, triggers, and procedures for activating and terminating the company's response plan, altering business operations (e.g. shutting down operations in affected areas), and transferring business knowledge to key employees.

SECTION 4: ALLOCATE RESOURCES TO PROTECT YOUR EMPLOYEES AND CUSTOMERS DURING A PANDEMIC

1. Provide sufficient and accessible infection control supplies (e.g. hand-hygiene products, tissues and receptacles for their disposal) in all business locations.

2. Enhance communications and information technology infrastructures as needed to support employee telecommuting and remote customer access.

3. Ensure availability of medical consultation and advice for emergency response.

SECTION 5: COMMUNICATE TO AND EDUCATE YOUR EMPLOYEES

1. Develop and disseminate programs and materials covering pandemic fundamentals (e.g. signs and symptoms of influenza, modes of transmission), personal and family protection and response strategies (e.g. hand hygiene, coughing/sneezing etiquette, contingency plans).

2. Anticipate employee fear and anxiety, rumors and misinformation and plan communications accordingly.

3. Ensure that communications are culturally and linguistically appropriate.

4. Disseminate information to employees about your pandemic preparedness and response plan.

5. Provide information for the at-home care of ill employees and family members.

6. Develop platforms (e.g. hotlines, dedicated websites) for communicating pandemic status and actions to employees, vendors, suppliers, and customers inside and outside the worksite in a consistent and timely way, including redundancies in the emergency contact system.

7. Identify community sources for timely and accurate pandemic information (domestic and international) and resources for obtaining counter-measures (e.g. vaccines and antivirals).

SECTION 6: COORDINATE WITH EXTERNAL ORGANIZATIONS AND HELP YOUR COMMUNITY

1. Collaborate with insurers, health plans, and major local healthcare facilities to share your pandemic plans and understand their capabilities and plans.

2. Collaborate with federal, state, and local public health agencies and/or emergency responders to participate in their planning processes, share your pandemic plans, and understand their capabilities and plans.

3. Communicate with local and/or state public health agencies and/or emergency responders about the assets and/or services your business could contribute to the community.

4. Share best practices with other businesses in your communities, chambers of commerce, and associations to improve community response efforts.

SOURCE: U.S. Department of Health and Human Services

APPENDIX 9:
INSURANCE COVERAGE
DISCUSSION FORM

 **Ready** Business
Prepare. Plan. Stay Informed.

Insurance Discussion Form

Open for Business Worksheet
Insurance Coverage Discussion Form

Use this form to discuss your insurance coverage with your agent. Having adequate coverage now will help you recover more rapidly from a catastrophe.

Insurance Agent: _____

Address: _____

Phone: _____   Fax: _____   Email: _____

INSURANCE POLICY INFORMATION

Type of Insurance	Policy No.	Deductibles	Policy Limits	Coverage (General Description)

Do you need Flood Insurance?   Yes __   No __

Do you need Earthquake Insurance?   Yes __   No __

Do you need Business Income and Extra Expense Insurance?   Yes __   No __

Other disaster-related insurance questions:

_____

_____

_____

_____

APPENDIX 10:
SELECTED PROVISIONS OF THE TERRORISM RISK INSURANCE ACT OF 2002 AND THE TERRORISM RISK INSURANCE EXTENSION ACT OF 2005

THE TERRORISM RISK INSURANCE ACT OF 2002 [H.R. 3210 – 107TH U.S. CONGRESS, PUB. L. NO. 107-297, 11/26/02]

TITLE I—TERRORISM INSURANCE PROGRAM

SEC. 101. CONGRESSIONAL FINDINGS AND PURPOSE.

(a) FINDINGS- The Congress finds that—

(1) the ability of businesses and individuals to obtain property and casualty insurance at reasonable and predictable prices, in order to spread the risk of both routine and catastrophic loss, is critical to economic growth, urban development, and the construction and maintenance of public and private housing, as well as to the promotion of United States exports and foreign trade in an increasingly interconnected world;

(2) property and casualty insurance firms are important financial institutions, the products of which allow mutualization of risk and the efficient use of financial resources and enhance the ability of the economy to maintain stability, while responding to a variety of economic, political, environmental, and other risks with a minimum of disruption;

(3) the ability of the insurance industry to cover the unprecedented financial risks presented by potential acts of terrorism in the United States can be a major factor in the recovery from terrorist attacks, while maintaining the stability of the economy;

(4) widespread financial market uncertainties have arisen following the terrorist attacks of September 11, 2001, including the absence of information from which financial institutions can make statistically valid estimates of the probability and cost of future terrorist events, and therefore the size, funding, and allocation of the risk of loss caused by such acts of terrorism;

(5) a decision by property and casualty insurers to deal with such uncertainties, either by terminating property and casualty coverage for losses arising from terrorist events, or by radically escalating premium coverage to compensate for risks of loss that are not readily predictable, could seriously hamper ongoing and planned construction, property acquisition, and other business projects, generate a dramatic increase in rents, and otherwise suppress economic activity; and

(6) the United States Government should provide temporary financial compensation to insured parties, contributing to the stabilization of the United States economy in a time of national crisis, while the financial services industry develops the systems, mechanisms, products, and programs necessary to create a viable financial services market for private terrorism risk insurance.

(b) PURPOSE- The purpose of this title is to establish a temporary Federal program that provides for a transparent system of shared public and private compensation for insured losses resulting from acts of terrorism, in order to—

(1) protect consumers by addressing market disruptions and ensure the continued widespread availability and affordability of property and casualty insurance for terrorism risk; and

(2) allow for a transitional period for the private markets to stabilize, resume pricing of such insurance, and build capacity to absorb any future losses, while preserving State insurance regulation and consumer protections.

SEC. 102. DEFINITIONS.

In this title, the following definitions shall apply:

(1) ACT OF TERRORISM-

(A) CERTIFICATION- The term 'act of terrorism' means any act that is certified by the Secretary, in concurrence with the Secretary of State, and the Attorney General of the United States—

(i) to be an act of terrorism;

(ii) to be a violent act or an act that is dangerous to—

(I) human life;

(II) property; or

(III) infrastructure;

(iii) to have resulted in damage within the United States, or outside of the United States in the case of—

(I) an air carrier or vessel described in paragraph (5)(B); or

(II) the premises of a United States mission; and

(iv) to have been committed by an individual or individuals acting on behalf of any foreign person or foreign interest, as part of an effort to coerce the civilian population of the United States or to influence the policy or affect the conduct of the United States Government by coercion.

(B) LIMITATION- No act shall be certified by the Secretary as an act of terrorism if—

(i) the act is committed as part of the course of a war declared by the Congress, except that this clause shall not apply with respect to any coverage for workers' compensation; or

(ii) property and casualty insurance losses resulting from the act, in the aggregate, do not exceed $5,000,000.

SEC. 103. TERRORISM INSURANCE PROGRAM.

(a) ESTABLISHMENT OF PROGRAM-

(1) IN GENERAL- There is established in the Department of the Treasury the Terrorism Insurance Program.

(2) AUTHORITY OF THE SECRETARY- Notwithstanding any other provision of State or Federal law, the Secretary shall administer the Program, and shall pay the Federal share of compensation for insured losses in accordance with subsection (e).

(3) MANDATORY PARTICIPATION- Each entity that meets the definition of an insurer under this title shall participate in the Program.

(b) CONDITIONS FOR FEDERAL PAYMENTS- No payment may be made by the Secretary under this section with respect to an insured loss that is covered by an insurer, unless—

(1) the person that suffers the insured loss, or a person acting on behalf of that person, files a claim with the insurer;

(2) the insurer provides clear and conspicuous disclosure to the policyholder of the premium charged for insured losses covered by the Program and the Federal share of compensation for insured losses under the Program—

(A) in the case of any policy that is issued before the date of enactment of this Act, not later than 90 days after that date of enactment;

(B) in the case of any policy that is issued within 90 days of the date of enactment of this Act, at the time of offer, purchase, and renewal of the policy; and

(C) in the case of any policy that is issued more than 90 days after the date of enactment of this Act, on a separate line item in the policy, at the time of offer, purchase, and renewal of the policy;

(3) the insurer processes the claim for the insured loss in accordance with appropriate business practices, and any reasonable procedures that the Secretary may prescribe; and

(4) the insurer submits to the Secretary, in accordance with such reasonable procedures as the Secretary may establish—

(A) a claim for payment of the Federal share of compensation for insured losses under the Program;

(B) written certification—

(i) of the underlying claim; and

(ii) of all payments made for insured losses; and

(C) certification of its compliance with the provisions of this subsection.

(e) INSURED LOSS SHARED COMPENSATION-

(1) FEDERAL SHARE-

(A) IN GENERAL- The Federal share of compensation under the Program to be paid by the Secretary for insured losses of an insurer during the Transition Period and each Program Year shall be equal to 90 percent of that portion of the amount of such insured losses that exceeds the applicable insurer deductible required to be paid during such Transition Period or such Program Year.

(B) PROHIBITION ON DUPLICATIVE COMPENSATION- The Federal share of compensation for insured losses under the Program shall be reduced by the amount of compensation provided by the Federal Government to any person under any other Federal program for those insured losses.

(2) CAP ON ANNUAL LIABILITY-

(A) IN GENERAL- Notwithstanding paragraph (1) or any other provision of Federal or State law, if the aggregate insured losses exceed $100,000,000,000, during the period beginning on the first day of the Transition Period and ending on the last day of Program Year 1, or during Program Year 2 or Program Year 3 (until such time as the Congress may act otherwise with respect to such losses)—

(i) the Secretary shall not make any payment under this title for any portion of the amount of such losses that exceeds $100,000,000,000; and

(ii) no insurer that has met its insurer deductible shall be liable for the payment of any portion of that amount that exceeds $100,000,000,000.

(B) INSURER SHARE- For purposes of subparagraph (A), the Secretary shall determine the pro rata share of insured losses to be paid by each insurer that incurs insured losses under the Program.

(3) NOTICE TO CONGRESS- The Secretary shall notify the Congress if estimated or actual aggregate insured losses exceed $100,000,000,000 during the period beginning on the first day of the Transition Period and ending on the last day of Program Year 1, or during Program Year 2 or Program Year 3, and the Congress shall determine the procedures for and the source of any payments for such excess insured losses.

(4) FINAL NETTING- The Secretary shall have sole discretion to determine the time at which claims relating to any insured loss or act of terrorism shall become final.

(5) DETERMINATIONS FINAL- Any determination of the Secretary under this subsection shall be final, unless expressly provided, and shall not be subject to judicial review.

(7) RECOUPMENT OF FEDERAL SHARE-

(A) MANDATORY RECOUPMENT AMOUNT- For purposes of this paragraph, the mandatory recoupment amount for each of the periods referred to in subparagraphs (A), (B), and (C) of paragraph (6) shall be the difference between—

(i) the insurance marketplace aggregate retention amount under paragraph (6) for such period; and

(ii) the aggregate amount, for all insurers, of insured losses during such period that are not compensated by the Federal Government because such losses—

(I) are within the insurer deductible for the insurer subject to the losses; or

(II) are within the portion of losses of the insurer that exceed the insurer deductible, but are not compensated pursuant to paragraph (1).

(B) NO MANDATORY RECOUPMENT IF UNCOMPENSATED LOSSES EXCEED INSURANCE MARKETPLACE RETENTION- Notwithstanding subparagraph (A), if the aggregate amount of uncompensated insured losses referred to in clause (ii) of such subparagraph for any period referred to in subparagraph (A), (B), or (C) of paragraph (6) is greater than the insurance marketplace aggregate retention amount under paragraph (6) for such period, the mandatory recoupment amount shall be $0.

(C) MANDATORY ESTABLISHMENT OF SURCHARGES TO RECOUP MANDATORY RECOUPMENT AMOUNT- The Secretary shall collect, for repayment of the Federal financial assistance provided in connection with all acts of terrorism (or acts of war, in the case of workers compensation) occurring during any of the periods referred to in subparagraph (A), (B), or (C) of paragraph (6), terrorism loss risk-spreading premiums in an amount equal to any mandatory recoupment amount for such period.

(D) DISCRETIONARY RECOUPMENT OF REMAINDER OF FINANCIAL ASSISTANCE- To the extent that the amount of Federal financial assistance provided exceeds any mandatory recoupment amount, the Secretary may recoup, through terrorism loss risk-spreading premiums, such additional amounts that the Secretary believes can be recouped, based on—

(i) the ultimate costs to taxpayers of no additional recoupment;

(ii) the economic conditions in the commercial marketplace, including the capitalization, profitability, and investment returns of the insurance industry and the current cycle of the insurance markets;

(iii) the affordability of commercial insurance for small- and medium-sized businesses; and

(iv) such other factors as the Secretary considers appropriate.

(8) POLICY SURCHARGE FOR TERRORISM LOSS RISK-SPREADING PREMIUMS-

(A) POLICYHOLDER PREMIUM- Any amount established by the Secretary as a terrorism loss risk-spreading premium shall—

(i) be imposed as a policyholder premium surcharge on property and casualty insurance policies in force after the date of such establishment;

(ii) begin with such period of coverage during the year as the Secretary determines appropriate; and

(iii) be based on a percentage of the premium amount charged for property and casualty insurance coverage under the policy.

(B) COLLECTION- The Secretary shall provide for insurers to collect terrorism loss risk-spreading premiums and remit such amounts collected to the Secretary.

(C) PERCENTAGE LIMITATION- A terrorism loss risk-spreading premium (including any additional amount included in such premium on a discretionary basis pursuant to paragraph (7)(D)) may not exceed, on an annual basis, the amount equal to 3 percent of the premium charged for property and casualty insurance coverage under the policy.

SEC. 104. GENERAL AUTHORITY AND ADMINISTRATION OF CLAIMS.

(a) GENERAL AUTHORITY- The Secretary shall have the powers and authorities necessary to carry out the Program, including authority—

(1) to investigate and audit all claims under the Program; and

(2) to prescribe regulations and procedures to effectively administer and implement the Program, and to ensure that all insurers and self-insured entities that participate in the Program are treated comparably under the Program.

(e) CIVIL PENALTIES-

(1) IN GENERAL- The Secretary may assess a civil monetary penalty in an amount not exceeding the amount under paragraph (2) against any insurer that the Secretary determines, on the record after opportunity for a hearing—

(A) has failed to charge, collect, or remit terrorism loss risk-spreading premiums under section 103(e) in accordance with the requirements of, or regulations issued under, this title;

(B) has intentionally provided to the Secretary erroneous information regarding premium or loss amounts;

(C) submits to the Secretary fraudulent claims under the Program for insured losses;

(D) has failed to provide the disclosures required under subsection (f); or

(E) has otherwise failed to comply with the provisions of, or the regulations issued under, this title.

SEC. 105. PREEMPTION AND NULLIFICATION OF PRE-EXISTING TERRORISM EXCLUSIONS.

(a) GENERAL NULLIFICATION- Any terrorism exclusion in a contract for property and casualty insurance that is in force on the date of enactment of this Act shall be void to the extent that it excludes losses that would otherwise be insured losses.

(b) GENERAL PREEMPTION- Any State approval of any terrorism exclusion from a contract for property and casualty insurance that is in force on the date of enactment of this Act, shall be void to the extent that it excludes losses that would otherwise be insured losses.

(c) REINSTATEMENT OF TERRORISM EXCLUSIONS- Notwithstanding subsections (a) and (b) or any provision of State law, an insurer may reinstate a preexisting provision in a contract for property and casualty insurance that is in force on the date of enactment of this Act and that excludes coverage for an act of terrorism only—

(1) if the insurer has received a written statement from the insured that affirmatively authorizes such reinstatement; or

(2) if—

(A) the insured fails to pay any increased premium charged by the insurer for providing such terrorism coverage; and

(B) the insurer provided notice, at least 30 days before any such reinstatement, of—

(i) the increased premium for such terrorism coverage; and

(ii) the rights of the insured with respect to such coverage, including any date upon which the exclusion would be reinstated if no payment is received.

SEC. 107. LITIGATION MANAGEMENT.

(a) PROCEDURES AND DAMAGES-

(1) IN GENERAL- If the Secretary makes a determination pursuant to section 102 that an act of terrorism has occurred, there shall exist a Federal cause of action for property damage, personal injury, or death arising out of or resulting from such act of terrorism, which shall be the exclusive cause of action and remedy for claims for property damage, personal injury, or death arising out of or relating to such act of terrorism, except as provided in subsection (b).

(2) PREEMPTION OF STATE ACTIONS- All State causes of action of any kind for property damage, personal injury, or death arising out of or resulting from an act of terrorism that are otherwise available under State law are hereby preempted, except as provided in subsection (b).

(3) SUBSTANTIVE LAW- The substantive law for decision in any such action described in paragraph (1) shall be derived from the law, including choice of law principles, of the State in which such act of terrorism occurred, unless such law is otherwise inconsistent with or preempted by Federal law.

(4) JURISDICTION- For each determination described in paragraph (1), not later than 90 days after the occurrence of an act of terrorism, the Judicial Panel on Multidistrict Litigation shall designate 1 district court or, if necessary, multiple district courts of the United States that shall have original and exclusive jurisdiction over all actions for any claim (including any claim for loss of property, personal injury, or death) relating to or arising out of an act of terrorism subject to this section. The Judicial Panel on Multidistrict Litigation shall select and assign the district court or courts based on the convenience of the parties and the just and efficient conduct of the proceedings. For purposes of personal jurisdiction, the district court or courts designated by the Judicial Panel on Multidistrict Litigation shall be deemed to sit in all judicial districts in the United States.

(5) PUNITIVE DAMAGES- Any amounts awarded in an action under paragraph (1) that are attributable to punitive damages shall not count as insured losses for purposes of this title.

(b) EXCLUSION- Nothing in this section shall in any way limit the liability of any government, an organization, or person who knowingly participates in, conspires to commit, aids and abets, or commits any act of terrorism with respect to which a determination described in subsection (a)(1) was made.

(c) RIGHT OF SUBROGATION- The United States shall have the right of subrogation with respect to any payment or claim paid by the United States under this title.

(d) RELATIONSHIP TO OTHER LAW- Nothing in this section shall be construed to affect—

(1) any party's contractual right to arbitrate a dispute; or

(2) any provision of the Air Transportation Safety and System Stabilization Act (Public Law 107-42; 49 U.S.C. 40101 note.).

(e) EFFECTIVE PERIOD- This section shall apply only to actions described in subsection (a)(1) that arise out of or result from acts of terrorism that occur or occurred during the effective period of the Program.

TITLE II—TREATMENT OF TERRORIST ASSETS

SEC. 201. SATISFACTION OF JUDGMENTS FROM BLOCKED ASSETS OF TERRORISTS, TERRORIST ORGANIZATIONS, AND STATE SPONSORS OF TERRORISM.

(a) IN GENERAL- Notwithstanding any other provision of law, and except as provided in subsection (b), in every case in which a person has obtained a judgment against a terrorist party on a claim based upon an act of terrorism, or for which a terrorist party is not immune under section 1605(a)(7) of title 28, United States Code, the blocked assets of that terrorist party (including the blocked assets of any agency or instrumentality of that terrorist party) shall be subject to execution or attachment in aid of execution in order to satisfy such judgment to the extent of any compensatory damages for which such terrorist party has been adjudged liable.

THE TERRORISM RISK INSURANCE EXTENSION ACT OF 2005
[S. 467 – 109TH U.S. CONGRESS, PUB. L. NO. 109-144, 12/22/05]

SEC. 2. EXTENSION OF TERRORISM RISK INSURANCE PROGRAM.

(a) Program Extension- Section 108(a) of the Terrorism Risk Insurance Act of 2002 is amended by

striking '2005' and inserting '2007'."

SEC. 4. INSURED LOSS SHARED COMPENSATION.

Section 103(e) of the Terrorism Risk Insurance Act of 2002 is amended—

(1) in paragraph (1)—

(A) by inserting 'through Program Year 4' before 'shall be equal'; and

(B) by inserting ', and during Program Year 5 shall be equal to 85 percent,' after '90 percent'; and

(2) in each of paragraphs (2) and (3), by striking 'Program Year 2 or Program Year 3' each place that term appears and inserting 'any of Program Years 2 through 5'."

SEC. 5. AGGREGATE RETENTION AMOUNTS AND RECOUPMENT OF FEDERAL SHARE.

(a) Aggregate Retention Amounts- Section 103(e)(6) of the Terrorism Risk Insurance Act of 2002 is amended—

(1) in subparagraph (B), by striking 'and' at the end;

(2) in subparagraph (C), by striking the period at the end and inserting a semicolon; and

(3) by adding at the end the following:

'(D) for Program Year 4, the lesser of—

'(i) $25,000,000,000; and

'(ii) the aggregate amount, for all insurers, of insured losses during such Program Year; and

'(E) for Program Year 5, the lesser of—

'(i) $27,500,000,000; and

'(ii) the aggregate amount, for all insurers, of insured losses during such Program Year.'.

(b) Recoupment of Federal Share- Section 103(e)(7) of the Terrorism Risk Insurance Act of 2002 is amended-(1) in subparagraph (A), by striking ', (B), and (C)' and inserting 'through (E)'; and

(2) in each of subparagraphs (B) and (C), by striking 'subparagraph (A), (B), or (C)' each place that term appears and inserting 'any of subparagraphs (A) through (E)'."

SEC. 6. PROGRAM TRIGGER.

Section 103(e)(1) of the Terrorism Risk Insurance Act of 2002 (15 U.S.C. note, 116 Stat. 2328) is amended—

(1) by redesignating subparagraph (B) as subparagraph (C); and

(2) by inserting after subparagraph (A) the following:

'(B) PROGRAM TRIGGER- In the case of a certified act of terrorism occurring after March 31, 2006, no compensation shall be paid by the Secretary under subsection (a), unless the aggregate industry insured losses resulting from such certified act of terrorism exceed—

'(i) $50,000,000, with respect to such insured losses occurring in Program Year 4; or

'(ii) $100,000,000, with respect to such insured losses occurring in Program Year 5.'".

APPENDIX 11:
DIRECTORY OF STATE INSURANCE
DEPARTMENTS

STATE	ADDRESS	TELEPHONE	FAX
ALABAMA	Alabama Department of Insurance, 201 Monroe Street, Suite 1700, Montgomery, Alabama 36104	334-269-3550	334-241-4192
ALASKA	Alaska Division of Insurance, 550 West 7th Avenue, Suite 1560, Anchorage, Alaska 99501-3567	907-269-7900	907-269-7910
ARIZONA	Arizona Department of Insurance, 2910 North 44th Street, Suite 210, Phoenix, Arizona 85018-7256	602-364-3100	602-364-3470
ARKANSAS	Arkansas Insurance Department, 1200 West 3rd Street, Little Rock, Arkansas 72201-1904	501-371-2600	501-371-2629
CALIFORNIA	California Department of Insurance, 300 Capitol Mall, Suite 1700, Sacramento, California 95814	916-492-3500	916-445-6552
COLORADO	Colorado Division of Insurance, 1560 Broadway, Suite 850, Denver, Colorado 80202	303-894-7499	303-894-7455
CONNECTICUT	Connecticut Department of Insurance, PO Box 816, Hartford, Connecticut 06142-0816	860-297-3800	860-566-7410

STATE	ADDRESS	TELEPHONE	FAX
DELAWARE	Delaware Department of Insurance, Rodney Building, 841 Silver Lake Boulevard, Dover, Delaware 19904	302-739-4251	302-739-5280
DISTRICT OF COLUMBIA	Department of Insurance Securities and Banking, 810 First Street N. E., Suite 701, Washington, DC 20002	202-727-8000	202-535-1196
FLORIDA	Florida Office of Insurance Regulation, 200 E. Gaines Street, Tallahassee, Florida 32399-0301	850-413-5914	850-488-3334
GEORGIA	Georgia Department of Insurance, 2 Martin Luther King, Jr. Drive, 704 West Tower, Atlanta, Georgia 30334	404-656-2056	404-656-4688
HAWAII	Hawaii Division of Insurance, 335 Merchant Street, Room 213, Honolulu, Hawaii 96813	808-586-2790	808-586-2806
IDAHO	Idaho Department of Insurance, 700 West State Street, 3rd Floor, Boise, Idaho 83720-0043	208-334-4250	208-334-4398
ILLINOIS	Illinois Division of Insurance, 320 West Washington St., 4th Floor, Springfield, Illinois 62767-0001	217-785-5516	217-524-6500
INDIANA	Indiana Department of Insurance, 311 W. Washington Street, Suite 300, Indianapolis, Indiana 46204-2787	317-232-2385	317-232-5251
IOWA	Iowa Division of Insurance, 330 E. Maple Street, Des Moines, Iowa 50319	515-281-5523	515-281-3059

STATE	ADDRESS	TELEPHONE	FAX
KANSAS	Kansas Department of Insurance420 S.W. 9th Street, Topeka, Kansas 66612-1678	785-296-3071	785-296-7805
KENTUCKY	Kentucky Office of Insurance, 215 West Main Street, Frankfort, Kentucky 40601	502-564-6027	502-564-1453
LOUISIANA	Louisiana Department of Insurance, 1702 N. 3rd Street, Baton Rouge, Louisiana 70802	225-342-5423	225-342-8622
MAINE	Maine Bureau of Insurance, 124 Northern Avenue, Gardiner, Maine 04345	207-624-8401	207-624-8599
MARYLAND	Maryland Insurance Administration525 St. Paul Place, Baltimore, Maryland 21202-2272	410-468-2090	410-468-2019
MASSACHUSETTS	Massachusetts Division of InsuranceOne South Station, 5th Floor, Boston, Massachusetts 02110	617-521-7794	617-521-7758
MICHIGAN	Michigan Office of Financial and Insurance Services (OFIS) Attn: Office of the Commissioner, 611 W. Ottawa, 3rd Floor, Lansing, Michigan 48933	517-373-0220	517-373-4870
MINNESOTA	Minnesota Department of Commerce, 85 7th Place East, Suite 500, St. Paul, Minnesota 55101-2198	651-296-5769	651-282-2568
MISSISSIPPI	Mississippi Insurance Department, 501 North West Street, 10th Fl., Jackson, MS 39201	601-359-3569	601-359-2474

STATE	ADDRESS	TELEPHONE	FAX
MISSOURI	Missouri Department of Insurance, 301 West High Street, Suite 530, Jefferson City, Missouri 65101	573-751-1927	573-751-1165
MONTANA	Montana Department of Insurance, 840 Helena Avenue, Helena, Montana 59601	406-444-2040	406-444-3497
NEBRASKA	Nebraska Department of Insurance, 941 O Street, Suite 400, Lincoln, Nebraska 68508	402-471-2201	402-471-4610
NEVADA	Nevada Division of Insurance, 788 Fairview Drive, Suite 300, Carson City, Nevada 89701-5753	775-687-4270	775-687-3937
NEW HAMPSHIRE	New Hampshire Department of Insurance, 21 South Fruit Street, Suite 14, Concord, New Hampshire 03301	603-271-2261	603-271-1406
NEW JERSEY	New Jersey Department of Insurance, 20 West State Street, CN325, Trenton, New Jersey 08625	609-633-7667	609-984-5273
NEW MEXICO	New Mexico Insurance Division, 1120 Paseo de Peralta, Santa Fe, New Mexico 87501	505-827-4601	505-476-0326
NEW YORK	New York Department of Insurance, 25 Beaver Street, New York, New York 10004-2319	212-480-2289	212-480-2310
NORTH CAROLINA	North Carolina Department of Insurance, 430 N. Salisbury Street, Raleigh, North Carolina 27603	919-733-3058	919-733-6495
NORTH DAKOTA	North Dakota Department of Insurance, 600 E. Boulevard, Bismarck, North Dakota 58505-0320	701-328-2440	701-328-4880

STATE	ADDRESS	TELEPHONE	FAX
OHIO	Ohio Department of Insurance, 2100 Stella Court, Columbus, Ohio 43215-1067	614-644-2658	614-644-3743
OKLAHOMA	Oklahoma Department of Insurance, 2401 NW 23rd St., Suite 28, Oklahoma City, Oklahoma 73107	405-521-2828	405-521-6635
OREGON	Oregon Insurance Division, 350 Winter Street NE, Room 440, Salem, Oregon 97301-3883	503-947-7980	503-378-4351
PENNSYLVANIA	Pennsylvania Insurance Department, 1326 Strawberry Square, 13th Floor, Harrisburg, Pennsylvania 17120	717-783-0442	717-772-1969
RHODE ISLAND	Rhode Island Insurance Division, 233 Richmond Street, Suite 233, Providence, Rhode Island 02903-4233	401-222-5466	401-222-5475
SOUTH CAROLINA	South Carolina Department of Insurance, 1201 Main Street, Suite 1000, Columbia, South Carolina 29202-3105	803-737-6227	803-737-6159
SOUTH DAKOTA	South Dakota Division of Insurance, Capitol Avenue, 1st Floor, Pierre, South Dakota 57501-3185	605-773-4104	605-773-5369
TENNESSEE	Tennessee Department of Commerce & Insurance, 500 James Robertson Parkway, 5th Floor, Nashville, Tennessee 37243-0565	615-741-6007	615-532-6934
TEXAS	Texas Department of Insurance, 333 Guadalupe Street, Austin, Texas 78701	512-463-6464	512-475-2005

STATE	ADDRESS	TELEPHONE	FAX
UTAH	Utah Department of Insurance, 3110 State Office Building, Salt Lake City, Utah 84114-1201	801-538-3800	801-538-3829
VERMONT	Vermont Department of Banking, Insurance, Securities & Health Care Administration, 89 Main Street, Drawer 20, Montpelier, Vermont 05620-3101	802-828-3301	n/a
VIRGINIA	Virginia Bureau of Insurance, 1300 East Main Street, Richmond, Virginia 23219	804-371-9694	804-371-9873
WASHINGTON	Washington Office of the Insurance Commissioner, 302 Sid Snyder Avenue SW, Suite 200, Olympia, WA 98504	360-725-7080	360-586-2018
WEST VIRGINIA	West Virginia Board of Risk & Insurance Management, 90 MacCorkle Avenue SW, Suite 203, South Charleston, WV 25303	304-766-2646	304-766-2653
WISCONSIN	Wisconsin Office of the Commissioner of Insurance, 125 South Webster Street, Madison, Wisconsin 53703-3474	608-266-3585	608-266-9935
WYOMING	Wyoming Insurance Department, 106 East 6th Avenue, Cheyenne, Wyoming 82002	307-777-7401	307-777-2446

SOURCE: National Association of Insurance Commissioners (NAIC)

APPENDIX 12:
U.S. SBA DISASTER BUSINESS LOAN
APPLICATION

U. S. Small Business Administration
DISASTER BUSINESS LOAN APPLICATION

OMB No. 3245-0017

FOR SBA INTERNAL USE ONLY

Physical Declaration Number		Filing Deadline Date	
Economic Injury Declaration Number		Filing Deadline Date	
FEMA Registration Number (if known)		SBA Application Number	

1. ARE YOU APPLYING FOR:

☐ **Physical Damage** -- *Indicate type of damage*

    ☐ Real Property   ☐ Business Contents

☐ **Economic Injury (EIDL)**

☐ **Military Reservist EIDL (MREIDL)**
(complete the following)

* Name of Essential Employee _____

* Employee's Social Security Number _____ - ___ - _____

PLEASE PROVIDE ALL INFORMATION OR DOCUMENTATION REQUESTED IN THE ATTACHED FILING REQUIREMENTS.

* For information about these questions, see the attached Statements Required by Laws and Executive Orders.

2. ORGANIZATION TYPE

☐ Sole Proprietorship   ☐ Partnership   ☐ Limited Partnership   ☐ Limited Liability Entity

☐ Corporation   ☐ Nonprofit Organization   ☐ Trust   ☐ Other: _____

3. APPLICANT'S LEGAL NAME	4. FEDERAL E.I.N. (if applicable)

5. TRADE NAME (if different from legal name)	6. BUSINESS PHONE NUMBER (including area code).

7. MAILING ADDRESS ☐ Business ☐ Home ☐ Temp ☐ Other _____

Number, Street, and/or Post Office Box	City	County	State	Zip

8. DAMAGED PROPERTY ADDRESS(ES)
(If you need more space, attach additional sheets.) ☐ Same as mailing address

Number and Street Name	City	County	State	Zip

9. PROVIDE THE NAME(S) OF THE INDIVIDUAL(S) TO CONTACT FOR:

☐ Loss Verification Inspection   ☐ Information necessary to process the Application

Name	Name
Telephone Number	Telephone Number

10. ALTERNATE WAY TO CONTACT YOU (ie., cell #, fax #, e-mail, etc.)

Cell # ☑ Fax # ☐ E-mail ☐ Other ☐ Cell # ☐ Fax # ☐ E-mail ☐ Other ☐

11. TYPE OF BUSINESS:	12. DATE BUSINESS ESTABLISHED:
13. UNDER CURRENT MANAGEMENT SINCE:	14. BUSINESS PROPERTY IS: ☐ Owned ☐ Leased
15. AMOUNT OF ESTIMATED LOSS: If unknown, enter a question mark	16. NUMBER OF EMPLOYEES:

17. IF YOU ARE A SOLE PROPRIETOR, ARE YOU A U.S. CITIZEN? ☐ YES ☐ NO

18. IF YOU HAVE ANY TYPE OF INSURANCE, PLEASE COMPLETE THE FOLLOWING:

Name of Insurance Company and Agent	
Phone Number of Insurance Agent	Policy Number

SBA Form 5 (01-05) Ref SOP 50 30

---

19. OWNERS (If you need more space attach additional sheets.)				Complete for each: 1) proprietor, or 2) limited partner who owns 20% or more interest and each general partner, or 3) stockholder or entity owning 20% or more voting stock.			
Name				Title/Office	% Owned 99900	E-mail Address	
SSN/EIN*	Marital Status	Date of Birth*	Place of Birth*	Telephone Number (including area code)			
Mailing Address				City		State	Zip
Name				Title/Office	% Owned	E-mail Address	
SSN/EIN*	Marital Status	Date of Birth*	Place of Birth*	Telephone Number (including area code)			
Mailing Address				City		State	Zip

* For information about these questions, see the attached Statements Required by Laws and Executive Orders.

20. For the applicant business and each owner listed in item 19, please respond to the following questions, providing dates and details on any question answered **YES**. (Attach an additional sheet for detailed responses.)

a. Has the business or a listed owner ever been involved in a bankruptcy or insolvency proceeding? ☐ Yes ☐ No

b. Does the business or a listed owner have any outstanding judgments, tax liens, or pending lawsuits against them? ☐ Yes ☐ No

c. Has the business or a listed owner ever been convicted of a criminal offense committed during and in connection with a riot or civil disorder or ever been engaged in the production or distribution of any product or service that has been determined to be obscene by a court of competent jurisdiction? ☐ Yes ☐ No

d. Has the business or a listed owner ever had or guaranteed a Federal loan or a Federally guaranteed loan? ☐ Yes ☐ No

e. Is the business or a listed owner delinquent on any Federal taxes, direct or guaranteed Federal loans (SBA, FHA, VA, student, etc.), Federal contracts, Federal grants, or any child support payments? ☐ Yes ☐ No

f. Does any owner, owner's spouse, or household member work for SBA or serve as a member of SBA's SCORE, ACE, or Advisory Council? ☐ Yes ☐ No

21. Is the applicant or any of the individuals listed in Item 19 currently, or have they <u>ever</u> been:

a) under indictment, on parole or probation; b) charged with or arrested for any criminal offense other than a minor motor vehicle violation, including offenses which have been dismissed, discharged, or not prosecuted; or c) convicted, placed on pretrial diversion, or placed on any form of probation, including adjudication withheld pending probation, for any criminal offense other than a minor motor vehicle violation? ☐ Yes ☐ No If yes, Name _____

22. PHYSICAL DAMAGE LOANS ONLY. If your application is approved, you may be eligible for additional funds to cover the cost of mitigating measures (real property improvements or devices to minimize or protect against future damage from the same type of disaster event). It is not necessary for you to submit the description and cost estimates with the application. SBA must approve the mitigating measures before any loan increase.
By checking this box, I am interested in having SBA consider this increase. ☐

23. If anyone assisted you in completing this application, whether you pay a fee for this service or not, that person must print and sign their name in the space below.

Name and Address of representative (please include the individual name and their company)

_____ (Signature of Individual) | _____ (Print Individual Name)

_____ (Name of Company) | _____ Phone Number (include Area Code)

_____ Street Address, City, State, Zip | _____ Fee Charged or Agreed Upon

Unless the NO box is checked, I give permission for SBA to discuss any portion of this application with the representative listed above. NO ☐

AGREEMENTS AND CERTIFICATIONS

On behalf of the undersigned individually and for the applicant business:

I authorize my insurance company, bank, financial institution, or other creditors to release to SBA all records and information necessary to process this application.

I give my permission to release information in connection with this application to Federal, state, local, or private organizations that provide relief for disaster related purposes.

I will not exclude from participating in, or deny the benefits of, or otherwise subject to discrimination under, any program or activity for which I receive Federal financial assistance from SBA, any person on grounds of age, color, handicap, marital status, national origin, race, religion, or sex.

I will report to the SBA Office of the Inspector General, Washington, DC 20416, any Federal employee who offers, in return for compensation of any kind, to help get this loan approved. I have not paid anyone connected with the Federal government for help in getting this loan.

All information in and submitted with this application is true and correct to the best of my knowledge. All financial statements submitted with this application fully and accurately present the financial position of the business. I have not omitted any disclosures in these financial statements. This certification also applies to any financial statements or other information submitted after this date. I understand that false statements may result in the forfeiture of benefits and possible prosecution by the U.S. Attorney General (reference 18 U.S.C. 1001 and/or 15 U.S.C. 645).

SIGNATURE		TITLE		DATE	
Sign in Ink					

GLOSSARY

ACTUAL EVENT—A disaster, either natural or man-made, that has warranted action to protect life, property, environment, public health or safety.

ALERT—Notification that a potential disaster situation is imminent exists or has occurred; usually includes a directive for personnel to stand by for possible activation

ALTERNATE SITE—An alternate operating location to be used by business functions when the primary facilities are inaccessible.

ALTERNATE WORK AREA—Recovery environment complete with necessary infrastructure.

APPLICATION RECOVERY—The component of Disaster Recovery that deals specifically with the restoration of business system software and data after the processing platform has been restored or replaced.

ASSEMBLY AREA—The designated area at which employees, visitors, and contractors assemble if evacuated from their building or worksite.

ASSET—An item of property and/or component of a business activity or process owned by an organization.

ANNUAL LOSS EXPOSURE—A risk management method of calculating loss based on a value and level of frequency.

BACKLOG—The amount of work that accumulates when a system or process is unavailable for a long period of time.

BACKUP DATA—A process by which data, electronic or paper based, is copied in some form so as to be available and used if the original data from which it originated is lost, destroyed or corrupted.

BACKUP GENERATOR—An independent source of power, usually fueled by diesel oil or natural gas.

BUSINESS CONTINUITY—The ability of an organization to provide service and support for its customers and to maintain its viability before, during, and after a business interruption event.

BUSINESS CONTINUITY MANAGEMENT TEAM—A group of individuals functionally responsible for directing the development and execution of the business continuity plan, as well as responsible for declaring a disaster and providing direction during the recovery process, both pre-disaster and post-disaster.

BUSINESS CONTINUITY PLAN—Process of developing and documenting arrangements and procedures that enable an organization to respond to an event that lasts for an unacceptable period of time and return to performing its critical functions after an interruption.

BUSINESS CONTINUITY STRATEGY—An approach by an organization that will ensure its recovery and continuity in the face of a disaster or other major outage.

BUSINESS CONTINUITY TEAM—Designated individuals responsible for developing, execution, rehearsals, and maintenance of the business continuity plan, including the processes and procedures.

BUSINESS IMPACT ANALYSIS—A process designed to prioritize business functions by assessing the potential financial and non-financial impact that might result if an organization was to experience a business continuity event.

BUSINESS INTERRUPTION—Any event, whether anticipated or unanticipated which disrupts the normal course of business operations at an organization's location

BUSINESS INTERRUPTION COSTS—The impact to the business caused by different types of outages, normally measured by revenue lost.

BUSINESS INTERRUPTION INSURANCE—Insurance coverage for disaster related expenses that may be incurred until operations are fully recovered after a disaster.

BUSINESS RECOVERY COORDINATOR—An individual or group designated to coordinate or control designated recovery processes or testing.

BUSINESS RECOVERY TEAM—A team responsible for maintaining the business recovery procedures and complying with the organization's business continuity management program.

BUSINESS RECOVERY TIMELINE—The approved sequence of activities required to achieve stable operations following a business interruption.

BUSINESS UNIT RECOVERY—A component of Business Continuity which deals specifically with the recovery of a key function or department in the event of a disaster.

CALL TREE—A document that graphically depicts the calling responsibilities and the calling order used to contact management, employees, customers, vendors, and other key contacts in the event of an emergency, disaster, or severe outage situation.

CASCADE SYSTEM—A system whereby one person or organization contacts others who in turn initiate further contacts as necessary.

CHAIN OF COMMAND—A series of command, control, executive, or management positions in hierarchical order of authority.

CHECKLIST—Tool to validate that tasks have been completed and resources are available, to report on the status of recovery.

CHECKLIST EXERCISE—A method used to exercise a completed disaster recovery plan.

COLD SITE—An alternate facility that already has in place the environmental infrastructure required to recover critical business functions or information systems, but does not have any pre-installed computer hardware, telecommunications equipment, communication lines, etc.

COMMAND CENTER—A physical or virtual facility located outside of the affected area used to gather, assess, and disseminate information and to make decisions to effect recovery.

COMMUNICATIONS RECOVERY—The component of Disaster Recovery which deals with the restoration or rerouting of an organization's telecommunication network, or its components, in the event of loss.

COMPUTER RECOVERY TEAM—A group of individuals responsible for assessing damage to the original system, processing data in the interim, and setting up the new system.

CONSORTIUM AGREEMENT—An agreement made by a group of organizations to share processing facilities and/or office facilities, if one member of the group suffers a disaster.

CONTACT LIST—A list of team members and/or key personnel to be contacted including their backups.

CONTINGENCY PLAN—A plan used by an organization or business unit to respond to a specific systems failure or disruption of operations.

CONTINGENCY PLANNING—Process of developing advanced arrangements and procedures that enable an organization to respond to an undesired event that negatively impacts the organization.

CONTINUITY OF OPERATIONS PLAN—A plan that provides guidance on system restoration for emergencies, disasters, mobilization, and for maintaining a state of readiness to provide the necessary level of information processing support commensurate with the mission requirements/priorities identified by the respective functional proponent.

CONTINUOUS AVAILABILITY—A system or application that supports operations which continue with little to no noticeable impact to the user.

CONTINUOUS OPERATIONS—The ability of an organization to perform its processes without interruption.

COORDINATE—To advance systematically an analysis and exchange of information among principals who have or may have a need to know certain information to carry out specific incident management responsibilities.

CORPORATE GOVERNANCE—The process by which the directors and officers of an organization are required to carry out and discharge their legal, moral and regulatory accountabilities and responsibilities.

CORPORATE RISK—A category of risk management that looks at ensuring an organization meets its corporate governance responsibilities, takes appropriate actions, and identifies and manages emerging risks.

CORRECTIVE ACTION—Improved procedures that are based on lessons learned from actual incidents or from training and exercises.

CORRECTIVE ACTION PLAN—A process implemented after incidents or exercises to assess, investigate, and identify and implement appropriate solutions to prevent repeating problems encountered.

COST BENEFIT ANALYSIS—A process that facilitates the financial assessment of different strategic business continuity management options and balances the cost of each option against the perceived savings.

CRISIS—A critical event, which, if not handled in an appropriate manner, may dramatically impact an organization's profitability, reputation, or ability to operate.

CRISIS MANAGEMENT—The overall coordination of an organization's response to a crisis, in an effective, timely manner, with the goal of avoiding or minimizing damage to the organization's profitability, reputation, and ability to operate.

CRISIS MANAGEMENT TEAM—A team consisting of key executives, key role players and the appropriate business owners of critical functions who are responsible for recovery operations during a crisis.

CRITICAL BUSINESS FUNCTIONS—The critical business support functions that could not be interrupted or unavailable for more than a mandated or predetermined timeframe without significantly jeopardizing the organization.

CRITICAL DATA POINT—The point in time to which data must be restored in order to achieve recovery objectives.

CRITICAL INFRASTRUCTURE—Physical assets whose incapacity or destruction would have a debilitating impact on the economic or physical security of an organization, community, nation, etc

DAMAGE ASSESSMENT—The process of assessing damage to computer hardware, vital records, office facilities, etc. and determining what can be salvaged or restored and what must be replaced following a disaster.

DATA BACKUPS—The copying of production files to media that can be stored both on and/or offsite and can be used to restore corrupted or lost data or to recover entire systems and databases in the event of a disaster.

DATA BACKUP STRATEGIES—Data backup strategies will determine the technologies, media and offsite storage of the backups necessary to meet an organization's data recovery and restoration objectives.

DATA CENTER RECOVERY—The component of Disaster Recovery which deals with the restoration of data center services and computer processing capabilities at an alternate location and the migration back to the production site.

DATA MIRRORING—A process whereby critical data is replicated to another device.

DATA PROTECTION—Process of ensuring confidentiality, integrity and availability of data

DATA RECOVERY—The restoration of computer files from backup media to restore programs and production data to the state that existed at the time of the last safe backup.

DATABASE REPLICATION—The partial or full duplication of data from a source database to one or more destination databases.

DECLARATION—A formal announcement by pre-authorized personnel that a disaster or severe outage is predicted or has occurred and that triggers pre-arranged mitigating actions.

DENIAL OF ACCESS—The inability of an organization to access and/or occupy its normal working environment.

DEPENDENCY—The reliance or interaction of one activity or process upon another.

DESK CHECK—One method of validating a specific component of a plan.

DISASTER—A sudden, unplanned catastrophic event causing unacceptable damage or loss.

DISASTER RECOVERY—The ability of an organization to respond to a disaster or an interruption in services by implementing a disaster recovery plan to stabilize and restore the organization's critical functions.

DISASTER RECOVERY PLAN—The management approved document that defines the resources, actions, tasks and data required to manage the technology recovery effort.

DISASTER RECOVERY PLANNING—The technical component of business continuity planning

ELECTRONIC VAULTING—Electronic transmission of data to a server or storage facility.

EMERGENCY—An unexpected or impending situation that may cause injury, loss of life, destruction of property, or cause the interference, loss, or disruption of an organization's normal business operations to such an extent that it poses a threat.

EMERGENCY CONTROL CENTER—The command center used by the Crisis Management Team during the first phase of an event.

EMERGENCY COORDINATOR—The person designated to plan, exercise, and implement the activities of sheltering in place or the evacuation of occupants of a site with the first responders and emergency services agencies.

EMERGENCY INCIDENT—An urgent need for assistance or relief as a result of an action that will likely lead to grave consequences.

EMERGENCY OPERATIONS CENTER—A site from which response teams/officials provide direction and exercise control in an emergency or disaster.

EMERGENCY PREPAREDNESS—The capability that enables an organization or community to respond to an emergency in a coordinated, timely, and effective manner to prevent the loss of life and minimize injury and property damage.

EMERGENCY PROCEDURES—A documented list of activities to commence immediately to prevent the loss of life and minimize injury and property damage.

EMERGENCY PUBLIC INFORMATION—Information that is disseminated primarily in anticipation of an emergency or during an emergency. In addition to providing situational information to the public, it also frequently provides directive actions required to be taken by the general public.

EMERGENCY RESPONSE—The immediate reaction and response to an emergency situation commonly focusing on ensuring life safety and reducing the severity of the incident.

EMERGENCY RESPONSE PLAN—A documented plan usually addressing the immediate reaction and response to an emergency situation

EMERGENCY RESPONSE PROCEDURES—The initial response to any event and is focused upon protecting human life and the organization's assets.

EMERGENCY RESPONSE PROVIDER—Includes state, local, and tribal emergency public safety, law enforcement, emergency response, emergency medical, including hospital emergency facilities, and related personnel, agencies, and authorities.

EMERGENCY RESPONSE TEAM (ERT)—Qualified and authorized personnel who have been trained to provide immediate assistance.

ENTERPRISE WIDE PLANNING—The overarching master plan covering all aspects of business continuity within the entire organization.

ENTRY-LEVEL FIRST RESPONDER—Entry-level first responders are defined as any responders who are not a supervisor or manager.

EQUIPMENT—The set of articles or physical resources necessary to perform or complete a task.

EQUIPMENT ACQUISITION—The process of obtaining resources to support operational needs.

ESCALATION—The process by which event related information is communicated upwards through an organization's established chain of command.

EVACUATION—The movement of employees, visitors and contractors from a worksite or building to a safe place in a controlled and monitored manner at time of an event.

EVENT—Any occurrence that may lead to a business continuity incident.

EXECUTIVE / MANAGEMENT SUCCESSION PLAN—A predetermined plan for ensuring the continuity of authority, decision-making, and communication in the event that key members of executive management unexpectedly become incapacitated.

EXERCISE—A people focused activity designed to execute business continuity plans and evaluate the individual and/or organization performance against approved standards or objectives.

EXERCISE AUDITOR—An appointed role that is assigned to assess whether the exercise aims / objectives are being met and to measure whether activities are occurring at the right time and involve the correct people to facilitate their achievement.

EXERCISE COORDINATOR—Individual responsible for the mechanics of running the exercise and keeping it focused within the predefined scope and objectives of the exercise as well as on the disaster scenario.

EXERCISE OBSERVER—An exercise observer has no active role within the exercise but is present for awareness and training purposes.

EXERCISE OWNER—An appointed role that has total management oversight and control of the exercise and has the authority to alter the exercise plan.

EXERCISE PLAN—A plan designed to periodically evaluate tasks, teams, and procedures that are documented in business continuity plans to ensure the plan's viability.

EXPOSURE—The potential susceptibility to loss.

EXTRA EXPENSE—The extra cost necessary to implement a recovery strategy and/or mitigate a loss.

FEDERAL—Of or pertaining to the Federal Government of the United States of America.

FILE SHADOWING—The asynchronous duplication of the production database on separate media to ensure data availability, currency and accuracy

FLOOR WARDEN—Person responsible for ensuring that all employees, visitors and contractors evacuate a floor within a specific site.

FORWARD RECOVERY—The process of recovering a database to the point of failure by applying active journal or log data to the current backup files of the database.

FULL REHEARSAL—An exercise that simulates a business continuity event where the organization or some of its component parts are suspended until the exercise is completed.

GAP ANALYSIS—A detailed examination to identify risks associated with the differences between business requirements and the current available recovery capabilities.

HARDENING—The process of making something more secure, resistant to attack, or less vulnerable.

HAZARD—Something that is potentially dangerous or harmful, often the root cause of an unwanted outcome.

HEALTH AND SAFETY—The process by which the well being of all employees, contractors, visitors and the public is safeguarded.

HIGH AVAILABILITY—Systems or applications requiring a very high level of reliability and availability. High availability systems typically operate 24x7 and usually require built-in redundancy to minimize the risk of downtime due to hardware and/or telecommunication failures.

HIGH-RISK AREAS—Areas identified during the risk assessment that are highly susceptible to a disaster situation or might be the cause of a significant disaster.

HOTSITE—An alternate facility that already has in place the computer, telecommunications, and environmental infrastructure required to recover critical business functions or information systems.

HUMAN CONTINUITY—The ability of an organization to provide support for its associates and their families before, during, and after a business continuity event to ensure a viable workforce.

HUMAN THREATS—Possible disruptions in operations resulting from human actions.

IMPACT—The effect, acceptable or unacceptable, of an event on an organization. The types of business impact are usually described as financial and non-financial and are further divided into specific types of impact.

INCIDENT—An occurrence or event, natural or human-caused, that requires an emergency response to protect life or property.

INCIDENT COMMAND SYSTEM—Combination of facilities, equipment, personnel, procedures, and communications operating within a common organizational structure with responsibility for the command, control, and coordination of assigned resources to effectively direct and control the response and recovery to an incident.

INCIDENT MANAGEMENT—The process by which an organization responds to and controls an incident using emergency response procedures or plans.

INCIDENT MANAGER—Commands the local emergency operations center reporting up to senior management on the recovery progress.

INCIDENT RESPONSE—The response of an organization to a disaster or other significant event that may significantly impact the organization, its people, or its ability to function productively.

INCIDENT-SPECIFIC HAZARDS—Anticipated events that may or may not occur that require coordinated response to protect life or property, e.g., pandemic flu, avian flu, etc.

INFORMATION SECURITY—The securing or safeguarding of all sensitive information, electronic or otherwise, which is owned by an organization.

INFRASTRUCTURE—The underlying foundation, basic framework, or interconnecting structural elements that support an organization.

INITIAL ACTION—The actions taken by those responders first to arrive at an incident site.

INITIAL RESPONSE—Resources initially committed to an incident.

INTEGRATED EXERCISE—An exercise conducted on multiple interrelated components of a business continuity plan, typically under simulated operating conditions.

INTERIM SITE—A temporary location used to continue performing business functions after vacating a recovery site and before the original or new home site can be occupied.

INTERNAL HOTSITE—A fully equipped alternate processing site owned and operated by the organization.

INTERSTATE—A region comprised of multiple states.

INTRASTATE—A region within a single state.

INVENTORY—An itemized list of current assets such as a catalog of the property or estate, or a list of goods on hand.

JURISDICTION—A range or sphere of authority.

JOURNALING—The process of logging changes or updates to a database since the last full backup.

KEY TASKS—Priority procedures and actions in a business continuity plan that must be executed within the first few minutes or hours of the plan invocation.

LEAD TIME—The time it takes for a supplier to make equipment, services, or supplies available after receiving an order.

LIAISON—A form of communication for establishing and maintaining mutual understanding and cooperation.

LIAISON OFFICER—The individual responsible for coordinating with representatives from cooperating and assisting agencies.

LOCAL GOVERNMENT—A county, municipality, city, town, township, local public authority, school district, special district, intrastate district, council of governments, regional or interstate government entity, or agency or instrumentality of a local government; an Indian tribe or authorized tribal organization, or in Alaska a Native village or Alaska Regional Native Corporation; a rural community, unincorporated town or village, or other public entity.

LOGISTICS/TRANSPORTATION TEAM—A team comprised of various members representing departments associated with supply acquisition and material transportation, responsible for ensuring the most effective acquisition and mobilization of hardware, supplies, and support materials.

LOSS—Unrecoverable resources that are redirected or removed as a result of a business continuity event.

LOSS ADJUSTER—Designated position activated at the time of a business continuity event to assist in managing the financial implications of the event.

LOSS REDUCTION—The technique of instituting mechanisms to lessen the exposure to a particular risk.

LOST TRANSACTION RECOVERY—Recovery of data destroyed or lost at the time of the disaster or interruption.

MANUAL PROCEDURES—An alternative method of working following a loss of systems.

MAJOR DISASTER—As defined under the Robert T. Stafford Disaster Relief and Emergency Assistance Act, a major disaster is any natural catastrophe (including any hurricane, tornado, storm, high water, wind-driven water, tidal wave, tsunami, earthquake, volcanic eruption, landslide, mudslide, snowstorm, or drought), or, regardless of cause, any fire, flood, or explosion, in any part of the United States, which in the determination of the President causes damage of sufficient severity and magnitude to warrant major disaster assistance to supplement the efforts and available resources of States, tribes, local governments, and disaster relief organizations in alleviating the damage, loss, hardship, or suffering caused thereby.

MISSION-CRITICAL ACTIVITIES—The critical operational and/or business support activities required by the organization to achieve its objectives.

MISSION-CRITICAL APPLICATION—Applications that support business activities or processes that could not be interrupted or unavailable for 24 hours or less without significantly jeopardizing the organization.

MITIGATION—The activities designed to reduce or eliminate risks to persons or property or to lessen the actual or potential effects or consequences of an incident.

MOBILE RECOVERY—A mobilized resource purchased or contracted for the purpose of business recovery.

MOBILE STANDBY TRAILER—A transportable operating environment, often a large trailer, that can be configured to specific recovery needs such as office facilities, call centers, data centers, etc.

MOBILIZATION—The activation of the recovery organization in response to a disaster declaration.

MOCK DISASTER—One method of exercising teams in which participants are challenged to determine the actions they would take in the event of a specific disaster scenario.

NATIONAL—Of a nationwide character, including the state, local, and tribal aspects of governance and policy.

NATIONAL DISASTER MEDICAL SYSTEM—A cooperative, asset-sharing partnership between the Department of Health and Human Services, the Department of Veterans Affairs, the Department of Homeland Security, and the Department of Defense.

NETWORK OUTAGE—An interruption of voice, data, or IP network communications.

OFF-SITE STORAGE—Any place physically located a significant distance away from the primary site, where duplicated and vital records may be stored for use during recovery.

OPERATIONAL RISK—The risk of loss resulting from inadequate or failed procedures and controls.

ORDERLY SHUTDOWN—The actions required to rapidly and gracefully suspend a business function and/or system during a disruption.

OUTAGE—The interruption of automated processing systems, infrastructure, support services, or essential business operations, which may result, in the organization's inability to provide services for some period of time.

PEER REVIEW—A review of a specific component of a plan by personnel with appropriate technical or business knowledge for accuracy and completeness.

PLAN ADMINISTRATOR—The individual responsible for documenting recovery activities and tracking recovery progress.

PLAN MAINTENANCE—The management process of keeping an organization's business continuity management plans up to date and effective.

PREPAREDNESS—The range of deliberate, critical tasks and activities necessary to build, sustain, and improve the operational capability to prevent, protect against, respond to, and recover from domestic incidents.

PREVENTATIVE MEASURES—Controls aimed at deterring or mitigating undesirable events from taking place.

PREVENTION—Actions to avoid an incident or to intervene to stop an incident from occurring.

PRIORITIZATION—The ordering of critical activities.

PRIVATE SECTOR—Organizations and entities that are not part of any governmental structure, including for-profit and not-for-profit organizations, formal and informal structures, commerce and industry, and private voluntary organizations.

PUBLIC INFORMATION OFFICER—The individual responsible for interfacing with the public and media or with other agencies with incident-related information requirements.

QUALITATIVE ASSESSMENT—The process for evaluating a business function based on observations.

QUANTITATIVE ASSESSMENT—The process for placing value on a business function for risk purposes.

RECIPROCAL AGREEMENT—Agreement between two organizations with similar equipment that allows each one to recover at the other's location.

RECOVERABLE LOSS—Financial losses due to an event that may be reclaimed in the future, e.g. through insurance or litigation.

RECOVERY—Implementing the prioritized actions required to return the processes and support functions to operational stability following an interruption or disaster.

RECOVERY PERIOD—The time period between a disaster and a return to normal functions, during which the disaster recovery plan is employed.

RECOVERY PLAN—A plan developed by a State, local, or tribal jurisdiction with assistance from responding Federal agencies to restore the affected area.

RECOVERY POINT OBJECTIVE—The maximum amount of data loss an organization can sustain during an event.

RECOVERY SERVICES AGREEMENT CONTRACT—A contract with an external organization guaranteeing the provision of specified equipment, facilities, or services, usually within a specified time period, in the event of a business interruption.

RECOVERY SITE—A designated site for the recovery of business unit, technology, or other operations, which are critical to the enterprise.

RECOVERY TEAMS—A structured group of teams ready to take control of the recovery operations if a disaster should occur.

RECOVERY TIME OBJECTIVE—The period of time within which systems, applications, or functions must be recovered after an outage.

RECOVERY TIMELINE—The sequence of recovery activities, or critical path, which must be followed to resume an acceptable level of operation following a business interruption.

RESILIENCE—The ability of an organization to absorb the impact of a business interruption, and continue to provide a minimum acceptable level of service.

RESILIENT—The process and procedures required to maintain or recover critical services such as "remote access" or "end-user support" during a business interruption.

RESOURCES—Personnel and major items of equipment, supplies, and facilities available or potentially available for assignment to incident operations and for which status is maintained.

RESPONSE—Activities that address the short-term, direct effects of an incident. Response includes immediate actions to save lives, protect property, and meet basic human needs. Response also includes the execution of emergency operations plans and incident mitigation activities designed to limit the loss of life, personal injury, property damage, and other unfavorable outcomes.

RESTORATION—Process of planning for and/or implementing procedures for the repair of hardware, relocation of the primary site and its contents, and returning to normal operations at the permanent operational location.

RESUMPTION—The process of planning for and/or implementing the restarting of defined business processes and operations following a disaster.

RISK—Potential for exposure to loss which can be determined by using either qualitative or quantitative measures.

RISK ASSESSMENT ANALYSIS—Process of identifying the risks to an organization, assessing the critical functions necessary for an organization to continue business operations, defining the controls in place to reduce organization exposure and evaluating the cost for such controls.

RISK CONTROLS—All methods of reducing the frequency and/or severity of losses including exposure avoidance, loss prevention, loss reduction, segregation of exposure units and non-insurance transfer of risk.

RISK MANAGEMENT—The culture, processes and structures that are put in place to effectively manage potential negative events.

RISK TRANSFER—A common technique used by risk managers to address or mitigate potential exposures of the organization.

ROLL CALL—The process of identifying that all employees, visitors and contractors have been safely evacuated and accounted for following an evacuation of a building or site.

SALVAGE & RESTORATION—The act of performing a coordinated assessment to determine the appropriate actions to be performed on impacted assets.

SECURITY REVIEW—A periodic review of policies, procedures, and operational practices maintained by an organization to ensure that they are followed and effective.

SELF INSURANCE—The pre-planned assumption of risk in which a decision is made to bear losses that could result from a business continuity event rather than purchasing insurance to cover those potential losses.

SERVICE CONTINUITY—The process and procedures required to maintain or recover critical services such as "remote access" or "end-user support" during a business interruption.

SERVICE CONTINUITY PLANNING—A process used to mitigate, develop, and document procedures that enable an organization to recover critical services after a business interruption.

SIMULATION EXERCISE—One method of exercising teams in which participants perform some or all of the actions they would take in the event of plan activation

SINGLE POINT OF FAILURE—A unique pathway or source of a service, activity, and/or process.

STAGING AREA—Location established where resources can be placed while awaiting a tactical assignment.

STANDARD OPERATING PROCEDURES—A complete reference document that details the procedures for performing a single function or a number of independent functions.

STAND DOWN—Formal notification that the response to a business continuity event is no longer required or has been concluded.

STANDALONE TEST—A test conducted on a specific component of a plan in isolation from other components to validate component functionality.

STRUCTURED WALKTHROUGH—Types of exercise in which team members physically implement the business continuity plans and verbally review each step to assess its effectiveness, identify enhancements, constraints and deficiencies.

SUPPLY CHAIN—All suppliers, manufacturing facilities, distribution centers, warehouses, customers, raw materials, work-in-process inventory, finished goods, and all related information and resources involved in meeting customer and organizational requirements.

SYSTEM—Set of related technology components that work together to support a business process or provide a service.

SYSTEM RECOVERY—The procedures for rebuilding a computer system and network to the condition where it is ready to accept data and applications, and facilitate network communications.

SYSTEM RESTORE—The procedures necessary to return a system to an operable state using all available data including data captured by alternate means during the outage.

TABLE TOP EXERCISE—One method of exercising plans in which participants review and discuss the actions they would take without actually performing the actions.

TASK LIST—Defined mandatory and discretionary tasks allocated to teams and/or individual roles within a business continuity plan.

TERRITORY—A geographical area belonging to or under the jurisdiction of a governmental authority.

TERRORISM—Under the Homeland Security Act of 2002, terrorism is defined as activity that involves an act dangerous to human life or potentially destructive of critical infrastructure or key resources and is a violation of the criminal laws of the United States or of any State or other subdivision of the United States in which it occurs and is intended to intimidate or coerce the civilian population or influence a government or affect the conduct of a government by mass destruction, assassination, or kidnapping.

THREAT—An indication of possible violence, harm, or danger.

TRAINING—Specialized instruction and practice to improve performance and lead to enhanced emergency management capabilities.

TRAINING CURRICULUM—A course or set of courses designed to teach personnel specific processes, concepts, or task-oriented skills.

TRAUMA COUNSELING—The provisioning of counseling assistance by trained individuals to employees, customers and others who have suffered mental or physical injury as the result of an event.

TRAUMA MANAGEMENT—The process of helping employees deal with trauma in a systematic way following an event by providing trained counselors, support systems, and coping strategies with the objective of restoring employees psychological well being.

UNEXPECTED LOSS—The worst-case financial loss or impact that a business could incur due to a particular loss event or risk.

UNINTERRUPTIBLE POWER SUPPLY—A backup electrical power supply that provides continuous power to critical equipment in the event that commercial power is lost.

VOLUNTEER—Any individual who performs services without promise, expectation, or receipt of compensation for services performed.

VALIDATION SCRIPT—A set of procedures within the business continuity plan to validate the proper function of a system or process before returning it to production operation.

VITAL RECORDS—Records essential to the continued functioning or reconstitution of an organization during and after an emergency including those records essential to protecting the legal and financial rights of that organization and of the individuals directly affected by its activities.

WARM SITE—An alternate processing site which is equipped with some hardware, and communications interfaces, electrical and environmental conditioning which is only capable of providing backup after additional provisioning, software or customization is performed.

WORK AREA FACILITY—A pre-designated space provided with desks, telephones, PCs, etc. ready for occupation by business recovery teams at short notice.

WORK AREA RECOVERY—The component of recovery and continuity that deals specifically with the relocation of a key function or department in the event of a disaster, including personnel, essential records, equipment supplies, work space, communication facilities, work station computer processing capability, fax, copy machines, mail services, etc.

WORK AREA RECOVERY PLANNING—The business continuity planning process of identifying the needs and preparing procedures and personnel for use at the work area facility.

WORKAROUND PROCEDURES—Alternative procedures that may be used by a functional unit(s) to enable it to continue to perform its critical functions during temporary unavailability of specific application systems, electronic or hard copy data, voice or data communication systems, specialized equipment, office facilities, personnel, or external services.

BIBLIOGRAPHY AND ADDITIONAL RESOURCES

American Red Cross (Date Visited: June 2007) http://www.redcross.org/services/disaster/.

Black's Law Dictionary, Fifth Edition. St. Paul, MN: West Publishing Company, 1979.

Disaster Recovery Journal (Date Visited: June 2007) http://www.drj.com/.

Federal Emergency Management Agency (Date Visited: June 2007) http://www.fema.gov/.

Insurance Information Institute (Date Visited: June 2007) http://www.iii.org/.

National Association of Insurance Commissioners (Date Visited: June 2007) http://www.naic.org/.

Occupational Health and Safety Administration (OSHA) (Date Visited: June 2007) http://www.osha.gov/.

U.S. Department of Homeland Security (Date Visited: June 2007) http://www.dhs.gov/.

The U.S. Environmental Protection Agency (Date Visited: June 2007) http://www.epa.gov/.

U.S. Small Business Administration (Date Visited: June 2007) http://www.sba.gov/.